Advan

"As an acting coach and former talent manager to hundreds of young performers nationwide, I am thrilled to have a concise, simple, and pragmatic book that I can recommend to my students about the world of vocal coaching and training. With years of experience and knowledge, Bob tells it like it is in his straightforward, to the point manner. His insight, wisdom, and passion for teaching make this book an invaluable resource for performers of any age. Having worked alongside Bob co-teaching classes for over 20 years, I can tell you he truly cares about the health and welfare of his students and their voices as a mentor, teacher, and coach."

– *Denise Simon*
Author of "Parenting in the Spotlight: How to Raise a Child Star Without Screwing Them Up"

"Bob Marks is a fantastic coach! His instincts for song selection and cuts are impeccable, but, most importantly, he knows how to take what you have to bring to the table, finesse it and help you be your best-prepared self in the audition room. Not to mention, he truly cares about his clients, their overall well-being, and is one of my dearest friends. I would not be where I am in my career without him!"

– *Stephanie Lynne Mason*
Broadway Performer

"I've known Bob for 40 years, ever since we attended college together, and I've watched him become one of the country's top vocal coaches, teaching some of Broadway's biggest stars. After college, I became a successful songwriter, writing for artists such as Barbra Streisand, Dolly Parton, and Vanessa Williams. Bob has often referred singer-songwriters to me to help them succeed in the music industry, and many of them have secured record and management deals in pop and rock music. With Bob's emphasis on vocal health, I always know that any singers I send him are in the best of hands. He is also one of the sweetest people I know. I will always be grateful for his friendship and support."

– *Lisa Ratner*
Songwriter, Producer, and Arranger

"My foremost memory of Bob Marks is back in 1979, when I was only seven years old. We walked into the backstage entrance of the Belasco Theatre together for my first Broadway audition. Bob accompanied me on the piano while I sang my audition song in front of director/ lyricist Martin Charnin and legendary composer Richard Rodgers. The show was a musical adaptation of *I Remember Mama*. Bob turned out to be my good luck charm, and I booked the role of Dagmar. My life was changed forever.

Fast forward... 34 years later. I never could have imagined that Bob would be an instrumental part of making my own child's show business dream come true. If it weren't for Bob's vocal lessons and coaching, my daughter Peyton Ella would never have been as prepared or confident during her audition process for NBC's *Sound of Music Live*, starring Carrie Underwood. Peyton landed the role of Gretl von Trapp from the open call audition, which I didn't want to bother attending. Bob convinced me that I should get right into Manhattan and give my daughter this opportunity. We are forever grateful for Bob's encouragement, friendship, and faith in his clients' abilities!"

– *Tara Kennedy*
Broadway Performer

"I learned so well from Bob. When I told him I was looking for an obscure piece of music, I was astounded when he said, "Wait a moment," and went to retrieve it from his library, and then proceeded to transpose it on the spot to a good key for me. Another time he gave me a song that literally no one had ever heard of, and that always got attention at auditions. His work is amazing."

– Jack Eppler
New York University Voice Faculty Member, Tisch School of the Arts

"I've been working with Bob for about 17 years. He is the best vocal coach, song arranger, and pianist I have ever worked with! He gave me the confidence to explore different genres of music that I would never have done on my own. Because of Bob, I went from just going for a weekly singing lesson to starring in my own cabaret show in NYC. I am proud to call Bob my coach, my musical director, but most of all, my dear friend!"

– Terri Troiano
Cabaret Performer

"Bob Marks' talent as a vocal coach, along with his extensive knowledge of music, is a gift for actors who love cabaret performance and song interpretation. He was an inspiration for me when I decided to sing publicly again after many years working behind the scenes with the incredible artistic and academic prowess of New York's pool of young performers."

– Alan Simon
Actor, Singer, Founder of On Location Education

"My daughter has had the good fortune to work with Bob Marks in both his NYC studio and in our hometown of Lexington, KY. His vast experience working with young singers has enabled him to develop a teaching style that is clear and efficient. This is significant for his students because it allows them to quickly understand and apply notes to their performance. He is a master at selecting repertoire and creating audition cuts that complete a musical thought while also highlighting the best parts of the performer's voice. We appreciate how his contribution to my daughter's training has helped her become more confident in and out of the audition room."

– Laura Nevels
Parent

"Bob Marks has artfully coached many of my students, written a couple of great articles for my *Popular Song and Music Theatre* column, and now has authored a wonderful book that is a 'must-read' for all of us in the business of singing. Thanks, Bob!"

– Robert Edwin
Singing Instructor, Associate Editor, NATS Journal of Singing

"I have worked professionally as a crossover singer/singing teacher and music theatre director in London, Paris, New York City, and Sydney for over 25 years. I used to commute to New York City from Paris to have lessons with Bob Marks. I was also lucky enough to have him come to Paris and work with my cast members, both in Master Classes and private lessons. Bob transformed my cast into a professional troupe! He knows the industry inside out and deeply understands what is needed to work, and gives practical, achievable, truly valuable insight and advice in what can be an overwhelming and confusing industry at times. His knowledge of music theatre is second to none. I wish I knew half of what Bob Marks knows about music, nuance, performance, and industry standards."

– Elizabeth Lecoanet
International Voice Specialist

"Bob Marks – a true legend. I think most people who have worked with Bob would agree. His warmth, talent, and caring just shine through all he does. I didn't study music or singing as much as I probably could have, but it was always a dream of mine to be in a big Broadway tour. My agents got me an audition for *The Lion King's* first national tour, and I was struggling to prepare, so I called Bob. His coaching was effective and to the point and really got me ready to go in a short amount of time. Bob was instrumental in helping me book the role of Ed the Hyena and the covers of Timon and Zazu in *The Lion King,* and I'm eternally grateful! After I was cast, I still needed/wanted coaching to learn all of the music quickly. Bob was able to get me in and out of his office, feeling confident that I could do what I needed to do to get the job done and be successful. Thank you, Bob Marks!"

– *Wayne Pyle*
Broadway Performer

"Bob Marks is a consummate professional in the musical theatre world. With a virtually encyclopedic knowledge of musical theatre repertoire and practice, he is a treasure trove of insight into the myriad of choices a singer has to make to create and explore their characters and roles. He is able to guide singers, from children to established professionals, so they find the unique qualities within that let them fully express their artistic potential."

– *Robert Doyle*
Voice Faculty, Albion College
Director of Choral Activities and Theatre
Dearborn Edsel Ford High School
International Clinician

"I have been a Broadway performer for nearly twenty years and always come home to Bob and his coaching for auditions. I am always prepared thanks to his professionalism, guidance, and expertise."

– Ben Lipitz
Broadway Performer

"About a year after moving to New York to pursue a career in acting, I thought it best to revisit singing. That's when I found Bob. Right from the start, I knew he was the right fit. I never mastered music theory or reading sheet music, but that didn't matter to Bob. He wanted to focus on what I wanted: a good voice. We've worked together for three years and counting, and during that time, he's stretched my voice from two octaves to three, helped me create a diversified bag of songs to fit any occasion, and, most of all, become a great friend of mine. Bob Marks really is the best vocal coach around!"

– William W Wallace
Actor

"When I re-entered the world of auditioning for musicals in my early 40s (after taking time off to raise my children), working with Bob Marks was the best thing that could have happened to my career! Instead of singing my ingenue repertoire from my early 20s, he steered me towards songs appropriate for roles I could actually be cast in. Now, I'm much more confident with my current selection of songs, which helped me land new roles which were more suited to my life experience."

– Audrey Heffernan Meyer
Professional Actor/Singer

Bob Marks'
88 KEYS TO SUCCESSFUL SINGING PERFORMANCES

AUDITION ADVICE FROM ONE OF AMERICA'S TOP VOCAL COACHES

By Bob Marks

and

Elizabeth Gerbi

THOMAS NOBLE BOOKS

Wilmington, DE

Author Contact: www.BobMarks.com, www.elizabethgerbi.com

Thomas Noble Books
Wilmington, DE
www.thomasnoblebooks.com

ISBN: 978-1-945586-31-6
First Printing: 2020
Bob Marks author photos by
Douglas Gorenstein Headshot Photography
www.DouglasGorenstein.com

This publication is designed to provide accurate and authoritative information regarding the subject matter covered. It is sold with the understanding that the author is not engaged in rendering professional services. If legal, accounting, medical, psychological, or any other expert assistance is required, the services of a competent professional person should be sought.

Dedicated to

The first singer I ever accompanied on the piano, my mother, Eve. She really taught me to follow the singer. And to my father, Peter, who struggled to pay for my piano lessons. He eventually got over my lack of enthusiasm for competitive sports. My grandmother Grete, a former violinist, who noticed that I could pick out tunes by ear on my toy piano. Also, my grandfather Paul, who took me to see a Broadway musical every year on my birthday.

My children and grandchildren, who continue to be my pride and joy.

My past, current, and former students, who really helped me learn most of what I know.

And, of course, my wife Elayne, who has put up with me for over 40 years. We met when I was hired as musical director of a regional production of *Hello, Dolly!* The director made me agree not to make her sing because she only wanted to dance. And all these years later, I've kept my word and never made her sing.

Table of Contents

Chapter 4: Mastering the Art of Auditioning

Chapter 5: The Accompanist

Chapter 6: Bringing Songs to Life at the Audition

Chapter 7: Audition FAQ

Chapter 8: Managing Your Career

Chapter 9: Your Continuing Education and Achieving Your Goals

Chapter 10: Encore!: Additional Resources

Prelude

When I began my journey as an agent almost forty years ago, many of the children who wanted to perform on Broadway were not being trained properly. *Annie* was a huge hit, and they were looking for replacements. Annie and the orphans had very demanding notes for girls' voices to sing correctly, up to a high F# in full belt. I was determined not to put a child in a position to do damage to her vocal cords. When I asked around, I was told that a new voice person was working with children in the city. And that is how I met Bob Marks. I immediately became a fan.

After *Annie* came *Oliver!* Then *Les Mis*, and on and on. As I began working with more and more actors of all ages, Bob's reputation continued to grow. He attracted a wide variety of performers looking for solid coaching with an emphasis on producing the sound correctly. In addition, Bob was providing solid advice and a support system for his students. It worked! More and more performers were listing Bob on their resumes and Broadway Playbill bios. His reputation soared.

I began wishing that he could be there for my many out-of-town singers needing the technique and teaching he offered. Finally, my wish has been answered. All I need to say is get a copy of "Bob Marks' 88 Keys to Successful Singing Performances." Now he's with you 24/7.

Thank you, Bob.
– Nancy Carson
Carson-Adler Agency, New York City

Overture

As of this writing, I have coached cast members of nearly every Broadway musical running today. First-time child actors, octogenarian actors, even the children of children I coached many years ago; all seem to show up at my studio at some time or another. When I started writing this book, I had just taught my 80,000th lesson. By the time I finished the first draft, I had crossed the threshold of my 90,000th and had learned so much in the intervening 10,000 hours that I felt like a new teacher!

Upon reflection, however, I realized that what is even more interesting than what has changed in the last five, ten, or forty years, is what has stayed the *same*. The actual act of learning to sing has remained remarkably unchanged since I began teaching. There is still the student and teacher, the sheet music, the piano, the person who plays, and the person who listens.

To better explain the work I do with my clients, let me shed a little light on my own background and how I happened to get into this business. Not having been a singer myself, it is a logical question to ask as to how I came to work exclusively with singers, much less ones as good as Debbie Gibson or Britney Spears or Hollywood actors like Sarah Jessica Parker and Natalie Portman.

Well, like a lot of children of the 1960s, I started taking piano lessons when I was very young, and music appeared to be one of the few things that came easily to me. My parents had always been avid theatregoers, and I was fortunate enough to see many shows. These included many of the classic hits of the Golden Age, like the original Broadway productions of *Hello, Dolly!* and *Fiddler on the Roof.* While I enjoyed what was happening on stage, I was mesmerized by the orchestra. It was particularly exciting to watch the conductor lead the players by expertly waving a baton.

When I turned 14, there was a sudden opening for a music director for an amateur theatre group mounting a production of *Damn Yankees.* Fourteen might strike some as remarkably young to land this kind of paying job, but since I played the piano and was very inexpensive, I landed the gig and figured out how to do it as I went along. Taking that early opportunity led to an offer to perform musical direction for other theatre groups, a summer camp, and even an off-Broadway show. When any of the performers from a show I was working on needed help preparing for a singing audition or performance, I was the person they called on. After all, I could afford to be inexpensive. I wasn't paying rent, so I charged only five dollars an hour!

A couple of years later, when I was 16 years old, my sister began taking voice lessons, and I went along with her to her first lesson. Her new teacher (the late and legendary Sue Seton) asked me what I did. I replied that I helped singers find and arrange their music and accompanied them on the piano. She responded, "So, you're a vocal coach?" I'd never heard the term before, but from then on, my five dollar an hour job had a name.

I began college as a music major, which seemed somewhat predestined. However, my interest in musical theatre pulled me towards the drama department, where I happily accompanied almost every class, singer, and musical production. Having little interest in the music department's two music choices (classical or jazz), I left school after my second year, only to return to college several years later, where I finally did get my degree in speech pathology. I wanted to learn more about the anatomy and physiology of the singing voice, phonetics, acoustics, and so much more. It turned out to be useful knowledge that I have used every day for the last forty years, helping me to keep singers of all ages and experience levels vocally healthy.

Today, I continue to work with every possible variety of student, from the Broadway actor seeking to hone and polish, to the fresh-faced beginner who's never heard of a larynx or a diaphragm. My students and I have experienced triumph, progress, and discovery, and it is those wonderful breakthrough moments that make the uphill trudge of repetition and practice all worth it. I wrote this book to provide students with some short, simple, measurable steps from which to start. I want to help them maximize the time they spend with their teachers, to help them know whether or not they're making progress, and to figure out those special things that they have to offer–those quirky, unique qualities that they or their agents might not know what to do with–and turn them into assets.

I'd be lying if I said it was all a cakewalk. Just as there are triumphs, so are there challenges. Some are small, needling problems, and some are big, imposing roadblocks. While trudging uphill, what happens when you can't quite seem to scale the mountain? Along this winding pedagogical road (sometimes paved, sometimes bumpy), I have worn many hats – cheerleader, psychologist, and even mind reader. However, being a singing coach, while not without its challenges, has always been intensely rewarding.

Being an effective singing coach requires a deep understanding not just of music and voice, but also of *people.* From a student's confining self-doubt to parentally-induced pressures, challenges radiate not just from technical limitations but also from an individual's preconceptions, environment, self-esteem, and personality. This book offers a peek at some of the more common, as well as the more confounding challenges that my students and I have faced in my career. By reading this, you will benefit by learning how to overcome these same struggles.

And always, no matter who you are, where you come from, or where you're going in this business, you can have a place in my studio, in person, or online!

– Bob

Chapter 1

Getting Started

1. Differences between singing *coaches* and singing *teachers*

In the past few years, the labels "singing coach" and "singing teacher" have been used interchangeably, although they used to mean quite different things.

A singing *coach* is someone who helps you with the overall musical and artistic shape of your performances. As in the world of sports, they pace in the dugout, cheer from the sidelines, encourage, strategize, motivate, and understand the intricacies of their players. Additionally, a good coach knows his player's vulnerabilities, both physical and mental, and makes it his or her job to minimize them.

A singing *teacher*, on the other hand, has traditionally been more concerned with the technical aspects of singing and is often a trained performer. They have a strong understanding of vocal anatomy and what's going on with the muscles, tissues, and ligaments underneath the surface of the skin. Moreover, they know how these connect with the body parts we can see, such as the tongue and jaw. A teacher will help the singer make adjustments to things within their control (mouth shape, breathing, volume, etc.) so they can optimize how the vocal folds produce sound. Also, good teachers are aware of the mind-body connection in a performer and will help students become more aware of how their thoughts and feelings affect voice production.

Traditionally, you went to a singing teacher to learn to sing in a healthy, beautiful way throughout your range with the hope of expanding that range. Alternatively, you went to a singing coach to achieve a stirring, communicative performance and maximize all of your vocal and dramatic assets over the course of learning new material.

In the past, a coach was someone who was concerned with presentation over technique, so they may have had little or no technical understanding of how the voice works. Similarly, a singing teacher often only studied classical music and would not be open to the sounds required for an authentic musical theatre performance. Only in recent years have colleges started offering degrees in all aspects of musical theatre and started graduating instructors who have both hands-on knowledge of theatre repertoire and training in how to help singers develop the right techniques to produce those sounds.

Nowadays, nearly all singing coaches must teach at least basic voice technique, while effective singing teachers will integrate expressive performance factors into their technical work. The ultimate goal is to help the performer cultivate a combination of skills and repertoire for effective and successful singing performances.

2. Find the right teaching professional to meet your goals

To grow as a singer, you need to know what you know, and, maybe even more importantly, become aware of what you *don't* know. To get you through it, the guidance of an experienced professional is invaluable.

New students are often afraid that a teacher or coach will tear them apart in the cheeky manner of some recent reality singing shows.

Do not confuse these made-for-TV sound bites for true coaching! The role of a coach or a teacher is to get to know you and inform you of your weaknesses in a useful, solution-oriented way. Teachers who pretend to know what they don't know can be quite destructive, sometimes more destructive to students' voices and overall confidence than if they never studied at all. Just like any other professionals, you will find some who are ego-driven (and possibly in the wrong area of work), some who are very sweet people but lacking in the know-how to help their clients achieve their goals, and some who are just right for your needs.

To achieve your true potential as a singer, you need to find knowledgeable coaches and teachers that you trust and be willing to listen to their advice. Even the best professionals can't know exactly what will happen at each audition. Still, their years of experience in the industry will offer a good vantage point and help you deal with the unexpected. I can only give advice based on my experience. Fortunately, I've been doing this for a long time, so my advice is often correct!

It's important to note that the relationship between different teachers and students is highly variable. A patient who is looking for counseling might fare better with a psychiatrist than a psychologist, and a client looking to get in shape might do better with an aggressive, "push-you-to-the-limit" kind of trainer, rather than a feelings-oriented life coach. In order to find what is best for you, you must make an honest assessment of your needs. When working with someone new, ask yourself:

- Does this teacher/coach use language that I understand?
- Does their advice make sense to me, and have they given me "homework" that I can do successfully on my own?

- Do they understand the types of sounds I want to make?

- How do I feel when I work with this person? Even if I'm nervous (very natural, especially at the beginning), do I feel respected, and that the teacher genuinely wants to help me?

- Do I sense that they are really listening and watching me?

- Are they asking for adjustments that make sense?

As we discussed earlier, teachers and coaches now often have overlapping skill sets. Ask yourself what your individual needs are. For example:

- Are you a brand-new singer or uncertain about singing? There are many teachers who specialize in working with new singers and welcome newcomers to their studios.

- Do you have a history of significant vocal problems, either physical (such as nodes, polyps, respiration issues, etc.) or psychological (music performance anxiety, PTSD) in origin? Then you probably want to find someone with advanced technical chops to help navigate through your problem areas.

- Are you a strong music reader, or do you play the piano? If not, you'll want to see someone who is also an accompanist so they can better prepare you for auditions.

- Are you trying to get work in a specific kind of genre such as a Gilbert and Sullivan operetta or a rock musical? Consider finding specialists in those areas who are familiar with those specific vocal and musical styles.

Don't be surprised if it takes more than one lesson for you to get a feel for your chemistry with a new teacher. It's just human nature that at first, both of you may end up trying to impress each other, so the atmosphere might not be as relaxed as it will be in the future.

However, if after a handful of lessons, you don't feel like you've found a good fit, it's probably best to listen to your gut and move on, so you have a better chance of finding the right match for you.

3. What to expect at your first singing lesson

Although every teacher is slightly different, any good teacher structures the first lesson around the needs of their clients. This is a time for me to get to know you better and start getting a sense of what sort of short and long-term goals you might have. In the days before an initial session, it's very helpful if you come up with a short mental (or written) list of concrete things you want to accomplish. Don't worry, these will change over time, but in the beginning, they offer a good launching point.

Some studios do require an audition for entrance or specialize in catering to the needs of particular populations, such as working Broadway professionals or child singers. A quick phone call prior to scheduling your first session will clarify the teacher's policies on this. However, unless the teacher states otherwise, teachers and coaches expect that all singers "come as they are," whether or not they have had any prior training or experience.

Expect a good amount of talking that first day, as I will be looking for clues in your speaking voice and personality as to how to best work with you. It's not that different from a job interview, where the interviewer is trying to get a "big picture" sense of the interviewee. Only in this case, your goal should not be to impress me. Be as honest and authentic as you can be in your responses to my questions.

If there are any specific materials I asked you to bring to the first day, like a recorder or songs from your repertoire, please bring those items with you. If you're not sure what I mean by a certain instruction or you don't have access to something, just let me know. It's fine if you'd like to record the session, although I like to be made aware of it.

Every session I do is structured around the specific needs of my clients. We usually begin with voice warm-up exercises for assessment as much as anything else. If these warm-ups reveal technique issues, I might go to some specific exercises that explore those and ask for some small adjustments to see how they affect the sound.

As far as repertoire goes, I like to hear a new client sing a song or two from his or her existing repertoire. To know where you're going, it helps to know where you've been. Obviously, if you have specific music to learn for an upcoming audition, that will be a priority.

Moving forward, sessions often include new repertoire for you to learn, exercises to help resolve technical voice issues, reviewing songs, and working on new arrangements or audition cuts. The main goal is to feel more confident and in control of your singing.

4. Create realistic goals

A lot of people seem to believe that the ability to sing well is somehow inborn and that singers fall into two camps: those with talent who practically come out of the womb singing beautifully and those who are tone-deaf (suffering from the medical condition *dysmelodia*), and shouldn't even bother trying to sing. The reality is that those are two dramatic extremes, which affect only a small handful of people. The other percent of us fall somewhere in the middle.

Just like any other art form, learning to sing well involves a great deal of time, practice, dedication, knowledge, and resources. I could probably sell a lot more books by promising you that there are "tricks" to singing that will turn anyone into a powerhouse performer overnight, but that is simply not true.

To be fair, it *is* true that a student with raw ability can make rapid progress with the right guidance. It is also true that some performers are late bloomers and must apply themselves over a long period before they make discernable improvement. However, the only "tricks" are the same healthy habits I impart to all performers: practice, study, and good vocal hygiene.

Because the process of singing is so unique to each person, at least some private study is critical for everybody. However, I am frequently amazed when a new client expects that a single lesson or two is enough for anyone to deliver a polished performance. If I gave trumpet lessons, no one would expect that, after one lesson, a student would be ready to audition for anything on a professional level!

When you go to a coach to prepare your songs, it's important to realize that it's not like buying a pair of shoes – you don't necessarily walk out with a song "ready to go." It is more like getting a suit tailored to your specific frame. Coaching is a process that not only involves choosing the right material, but also arranging and transposing the music as well as working on the performance vocally and physically.

How often you need to study depends on your schedule, your financial resources, and your goals. Consistency is important, especially at the beginning of private study. Once-a-week sessions are the norm, but it is not uncommon for clients to come in more often when important auditions come up, or they need to prepare for a callback. More experienced students with a solid practice regimen might find they come in less frequently for "check-ups" or to update their repertoire.

As an experienced coach, I have a fairly good sense of what can be accomplished on a given timetable, although bear in mind that results will vary for every individual!

In your first lesson, we need to get acquainted. I can lead you through warm-ups, get a sense of your strengths and weaknesses, and run through a couple of pieces you already know. I will try to bring your attention to small changes (where to breathe, diction issues, etc.).

After a month of lessons, we start to get into a rhythm with your practicing and will start to make headway with several new pieces of repertoire. With applied practice, you should feel at least small changes in your instrument.

After six months of regular study, most likely, you will notice a few major technical improvements in your singing. Depending on how much time you dedicate to practicing, you may have mastered a dozen or more songs in this time. Your instrument will start beginning to feel more "in-shape", and bigger changes in range, quality, and endurance should be obvious.

Of course, the results you achieve will depend in large part on the quality and time you put into practicing and where your natural strengths lie. If you are an exceptionally light soprano, it might take you longer to get your chest voice working than someone who has a more substantial voice and has already sung some belt repertoire.

Chapter 2

Health and Hygiene

5. Understand the basics of how your voice works

There are some conflicting opinions among singing teachers about how much you need to know about the biological and physical mechanics of making sound. Although it is true that you don't need to be an expert mechanic to drive a car, you are a more independent and a safer driver if you know basics of car maintenance, such as how to check oil and tire pressure before you set off on a marathon road trip. Also, knowing what a car should feel like when you are driving safely in gear will alert you to much bigger problems earlier on and save a lot on new transmissions! This is a case where I think a little vetted information goes a long way in preventing injury and expediting progress.

The actual source of the voice, the *vocal folds* (sometimes referred to as "vocal cords"), are a bit of a mystery to most people because they are hidden within the muscles and tissues of the neck. The vocal folds in humans are located within the *larynx* (pronounced "lair-inks"), sometimes known as the *voice box*, which is a small, walnut-sized organ situated at the top of your windpipe and below your jaw. The larynx has two main functions in the body: sound production and airflow. It also serves to prevent food and liquid from passing into the lungs when you swallow.

When speaking or singing (making sound, or, a more technical term, *phonating*), the vocal folds come together and create vibrations. You can feel this happen if you place your fingers on the top of your neck beneath your jaw and hum. Notice the vibrations? Now, notice when you stop to take a breath that the vibrations stop. That is because the vocal folds parted, allowing the lungs to become refilled with air. Just like it is essential for your car to have adequate fuel to make it to your destination, when singing, it's important to have sufficient airflow through the vocal folds to create the particular sound you desire. Learning specific breathing techniques can be extremely helpful for singing, especially intercostal ("between the ribs") breathing.

The muscles surrounding the vocal folds change pitch by increasing or decreasing tension. If you pluck a rubber band, the pitch rises as the band is stretched and lowers when tension is diminished. The vocal folds behave similarly: the thinner and longer they are, the higher the pitch. When the folds are thick and short, they produce a pitch that is lower. Minimizing excess tension in the throat should be one of the main focuses of voice lessons, particularly when singing higher pitches.

The third contributor to how your voice sounds, sometimes referred to as the "filters," include your nasal passages, oral cavity, and throat – basically, the open spaces above your vocal folds. The sounds produced by the vocal folds alone create a metallic, harsh buzz, a lot like a duck call used by hunters. This is where the power of your instrument comes from. Like the body of an exquisitely crafted violin, the filters shape and magnify certain qualities in the sound, which enhance the beauty and clarity of the sound, leaving us with the "complete" voice.

In a voice lesson, you will work all three aspects of production:

1. How the body manages the breath
2. How efficiently the vocal folds are creating sound (phonating)
3. How well all your filters are working to shape the sound

Often, you'll find that a deficiency in one aspect of the system quickly causes problems in the other two.

6. Common misconceptions about singing

When you consider how many hundreds of small muscular contractions are involved, the fact that most people can instinctively use their breathing muscles, vocal folds, and filters for speaking is pretty remarkable. This is in large part thanks to our brain, which takes care of a lot of our bodily functions, so we don't need to be consciously aware of them. Unfortunately, our voice's ability to run on autopilot may leave us thinking that our voice is operated by some sort of magical element, leaving us unaware of harmful habits.

Because most people never get a chance to see how their voice operates in an MRI or through a stroboscopy (the method an ENT doctor uses to examine your vocal folds by inserting a camera through the nose or mouth and using a strobe light to take individual images of our lightning-fast vibrating folds in motion), it is very easy for us to accept misinformation about how the voice works. This is understandable; if you'd never looked under the hood of your car, you'd probably have difficulty picturing how that works, too!

Here are a few common misconceptions that I run into frequently:

"Sing from your diaphragm." The diaphragm is a narrow, double dome-shaped muscle of inhalation that sits underneath the floor of your lungs and ribcage. It is actually passive on exhalation, meaning we can't

"use it" to make sound. It is frequently confused with the abdominal or intercostal muscles, which are used to help manage the release of air.

"To fix _____ about your singing, you need more air." Not always. You need the right amount of air, which may be more or less than you are using. For example, when singers have an overly breathy quality, they might be told to use more air to increase the amount of power in their sound. However, in this case, more air will just cause the vocal folds to blow apart, worsening the problem.

"You need to open your mouth more." You need to have the right-sized space for the sound you want, which may be larger or smaller than another singer based on the unique qualities of your voice. It is a very individualized process.

"You should start with the study of classical music, which will prepare you for all types of singing." The truth is, singers get injured in both classical and non-classical styles if they go too high, too long, or too loud for their current level of development. However, it is absolutely possible to sing beautifully and sustainably in all styles of music without having sung a note of classical repertoire.

It's important to study with someone who understands all aspects of the voice, regardless of whether he or she is a performing singer. Knowledge of anatomy, physiology, phonetics, as well as music will help you explore the direct link between how you breathe, phonate, and shape your singing voice.

7. Understand the basics of registration

If you want to see a group of voice teachers and voice scientists turn from a generally gregarious and collegial group into an angry mob, ask them to strictly define vocal registers or the "gears" of the voice that are responsible for different types of sounds.

If you study with a handful of different teachers, for example, they may refer to singing with thickened vocal folds as chest voice, modal voice, *voix I*, thyroarytenoid-dominant production, yelling, or speech-like production, just to name a few. Similarly, we might call sounds created with thin vocal folds: head voice, *voix II*, cricothyroid-dominant production, loft voice, falsetto, and on and on.

The fact of the matter is that it doesn't matter what you call these sounds. Whether you call those sounds chest, mix, head, or applesauce, has no bearing, as long as you are able to understand and recreate the results in a healthy way. On Broadway, what matters most is:

1. Does it sound right for the style of the show?

2. Does it sound appropriate for the character?

3. Is it produced healthily and sustainably?

"Theatre" as a category encompasses an enormous array of musical styles, requiring the singer to have to employ many different vocal modalities across their career. For example, a singer might be cast in a classic "Golden Age" style show such as *Carousel*, and then later sing a whole tribute program to Billie Holiday *(Lady Day at Emerson's Bar and Grill)*; and, if you are Audra McDonald, you might do this so skillfully that you earn Tony Awards for both. There is no question that versatility pays big dividends in this business.

Singers learn how to deal with these demands by becoming skilled in using the different available gears of their voice both at the source (the vocal folds) and adjusting the filters to create the exact sound that they want. There are only so many parameters of the voice under our control. Our job is to "mix" the qualities to create the right sound for a character, much like a painter might use colors. I will often ask a client to share with me the terms that they use to think about their voice, and then I will use those personal terms when working with them.

In the world of Broadway shows, singers often audition for many styles of musicals. Appropriate vocal adjustments can make all the difference when you have to sing for a traditional Rodgers and Hammerstein show one week and a rock musical the next. Regardless of what actual terms you and your teacher use to label vocal qualities, I recommend that you think of your singing in terms of actual sounds rather than value judgments such as "better" or "worse." An important ingredient for Broadway employment is versatility.

8. The importance of posture in singing

If you have ever attended a classical voice recital, you probably saw an elegantly dressed performer situated near the crook of a grand piano for the duration of the performance. Traditionally, recitalists remain standing with "noble" posture throughout their program and only gesture with their hands and body for extreme emphasis.

However, in musical theatre performances, singers are rarely given the opportunity to simply stand and sing. In fact, if cast in a show, you might be asked to do almost anything while you sing, from perform an elaborate dance routine to literally hang upside-down suspended by cables.

To keep your voice functioning optimally, you will want to practice singing in the most efficient manner possible, so your body gets used to what "ideal conditions" feel like. For most people, this means learning to stand in a tall, relaxed, balanced way. This allows you to make a habit of easy, unrestricted breathing and phonation, so when you step out on stage and are thinking about a thousand other things, your voice will still reflexively work the way you want it to.

Good posture allows your lungs to expand and contract more easily and prevents unnecessary tension in your neck and jaw. For most people, standing with feet about shoulder-width apart is a great place to start from. You want to appear comfortable, confident, and relaxed.

It is also an undeniable fact that singing is a visual art form. Freedom in the body translates to freedom of expression for actors. Your alignment will tell an audience a lot about you before you even open your mouth. Actors with good posture can breathe, move, and gesture in a much more organic and appealing way, regardless of whether they are playing a character with restricted movement or have to move in a large, dramatic fashion.

Many performers have had helpful results with movement-based practices such as Yoga, the Alexander Technique, or Feldenkrais®. Your whole body contributes to the ease of your voice's operation. Your voice teacher should be able to recommend options you can try for correction of imbalances and to strengthen the right muscles for the job.

9. Protecting your voice from unsafe demands

When I was serving as one of the pianists for the original Broadway production of *Annie*, many voice teachers shared with me that they were horrified little girls were being asked to belt out songs such as "Tomorrow" and "Hard Knock Life." And yet, some of these teachers refused to accept those young girls as students! At that time, many voice teachers would not agree to teach students who had unchanged, prepubescent voices. They were under the impression that voice lessons could permanently damage a child's voice, which remained a widely accepted belief for many years.

I didn't agree. Even then, my feeling was that if children were going to sing at auditions and performances, why not have them do it in the healthiest way possible? Why wait for puberty to learn good singing habits? In my experience, proper breathing, minimizing throat tension, and putting songs in appropriate keys produced healthy, educated singers as young as six years old.

Children's voices can indeed be deceptively hardy and, in some cases, require a bit of policing to make sure that vocal roughhousing – whether it be on the sports field, cheerleading practice, or play rehearsal – is kept within very manageable limits. However, as long as we are teaching them healthy production habits and keeping an eye out for any indication of doing too much too soon, children often delight in singing on stage.

As their bodies change, both males and females endure a major vocal overhaul, although the female voice change is typically not as acute. Male vocal folds may increase by over two times that of the female, resulting in a singing voice a full octave lower than prior to the voice change. In both cases, changes in coordination, like the sudden inability to match certain pitches, may emerge, and singing might temporarily become much more difficult. Obviously, it makes sense that any voice professional would use extreme caution when working with a child singer.

A newer issue that has gained more attention in recent years is the question of how to best support aging voices through transitions that parallel adolescence in scope and intensity. Pregnancy, menopause, significant weight gain or loss, the addition or subtraction of certain medications and endocrine conditions are examples of hormonal changes that can wreak havoc on adult voices. Adults who are unwilling to change their decades-long approach to singing can be just as prone to potential injury as small children. However, aging singers can often find new and captivating expressive assets in their instruments if they embrace their changing voices.

Nowadays, many qualified teachers and coaches are helping their students develop healthy, contemporary singing technique in all vocal registers and at all ages. These specialists have a great deal of experience with and respect for the limitations of both young and aging voices. Only nature determines how quickly the voice changes and compensatory key adjustments to songs may need to be made to repertoire as the vocal range morphs.

A teacher or coach should help you to sound as good as possible. I treat all of my clients with the same honesty and respect regardless of their chronological age while continuing to stress healthy vocal production. Over the years, I've taught students of all ages and welcome the diversity, but vocal health is always my main emphasis. As the physician's Hippocratic Oath states, "First, do no harm," and I believe this is a promise that is vital in any teaching situation.

For more tips on keeping your voice in top shape, see Chapter 10 for some valuable pointers from Dr. Wendy LeBorgne.

10. Consider your performance goals in the context of your lifestyle

Professional singing is a very competitive industry, and it takes a great deal of self-discipline to maintain a career.

The vocal mechanism is extremely delicate and can be easily injured. Frequent yelling, shouting, whispering (believe it or not, this is more taxing on the voice than speaking at a conversational volume), constant throat clearing, and many other behaviors can lead to voice problems. Trying to speak over loud music at clubs or general crowd noise while working a bar or restaurant job can also hurt the voice. Many vocal injuries are from overuse, which can involve any kind of excessive vocalizing, whether that be speaking or singing.

Voice problems are not, however, always due to abuse. Illness can also lead to hoarseness or loss of voice and can greatly exacerbate the effects of even small amounts of overuse. To avoid complications, singers must deal with allergies, as well as digestive, respiratory, and dental problems as soon as they emerge. Your instrument involves quite a bit of upkeep, and you have to factor these items into your budget and lifestyle. A couple of ignored dental appointments or failure to follow your doctor's GERD (gastroesophageal reflux disease) diet, for example, can easily escalate to conditions that will leave your voice out of commission for weeks or months.

Unfortunately, your voice can also experience wear and tear when you are at play; any activity that consistently leaves you hoarse and unable to recover by the next day needs to be reconsidered. This applies to everything you do, from children's sleepovers to Friday night corporate mixers. If your voice shows signs of wear the next day, you can't afford to do that thing regularly.

I think the average person would be surprised at how much time and effort working singers invest in their vocal health. For Broadway singers to handle eight shows a week, they must practice daily while spending most of their non-performing hours on vocal rest, sleep adequately, be constantly hydrated, develop immune systems of steel, and stay in immaculate physical shape. Many actors find that they have to sacrifice a great deal of ordinary social life to meet these demands.

The good news is that the things that are great for your voice are also extremely beneficial for your general health. Very few lives suffer from good nutrition, adequate rest, hydration, and clean living, and regardless of whether you want to sing in the church choir or on a national tour, your voice and body will provide bountiful returns on your health investment. However, for a working singer, it's not a choice!

11. Care and feeding of your vocal instrument

The same principles that lead to sound vocal hygiene also promote a clear mind, better energy, and enhanced overall quality of life. Proper care of your voice doesn't require you to live much differently than you would for a normal, healthy lifestyle with a balanced and holistic approach.

Make sure you drink plenty of water. Keeping the throat moist will help minimize coughing and throat clearing by thinning out the mucus covering your vocal folds. You need this mucus to make your folds slippery and resistant to overuse. Still, sometimes this layer also becomes unusually thick or viscous due to other factors, such as allergies, dietary sensitivities, or hormonal shifts in your body. Chat with your doctor if you are not sure how much water to drink, as this can be affected by your age, activity level, and the climate that you live in. Remember, too, that your "inside environment" can also affect hydration levels; be sure to take extra care if you live and work in overly heated or air-conditioned spaces, or if you fly often.

Get enough rest. This includes getting quality sleep and enough vocal and physical downtime to allow muscles and tissues to repair themselves. When you are not getting enough rest to recover from daily stresses, your voice will pay the price.

Your diet can be even trickier to sort out. You must experiment and learn what healthy eating is for you, which may be very different from your family, friends, or even your voice teacher. Your body has a dynamic response to foods, and you might find that foods you could once handle now have strange effects on your body and voice at different times in your life. Practice dietary mindfulness and take your body's unique reaction to foods much more seriously than "rules" other singers pass on to you, such as to never eat dairy before singing.

Some questions to consider:

- Are you prone to acid reflux (usual suspects: vinegars, citric acid, carbonation, caffeine, citrus, tomato, chocolate, alcohol, peppermint, very fatty or spicy foods) or have known allergies, sensitivities, or inflammatory responses to certain foods (common triggers: soy, gluten, corn, dairy, eggs, sugar, chocolate, peanuts, tree nuts)?

- Do certain foods or additives, like caffeine, sugar, or MSG cause you anxiety or make it harder for you to focus?

- Which foods are truly "easy on your digestion," and which should you avoid before singing based on how you feel?

- How does the timing of your meals affect your voice? Does eating or drinking late at night (within three hours of bed) exacerbate reflux symptoms for you?

- How soon should you eat before an important audition or rehearsal to perform at your best? How much and how often do you need to eat and drink to feel optimally fueled?

- What eating habits allow you to be the healthiest weight and leanest body mass for your physical frame?

Of course, you should always talk to your doctor before making major changes. However, you can safely observe how your regular diet affects your performance at any time and err for the healthier option whenever given the choice.

12. Take precautions

If your overall health isn't good, your voice will probably not be in optimal shape either. There are a lot of small actions you can take that can help both your voice and your body stay healthy. For example, washing hands has been shown to reduce viral colds. Try to bear this in mind, especially when in cold and flu season or when spending a lot of time in contained, public places like schools, airplanes, buses, and shopping centers. Also, avoid touching your nose and face with your hands if you live or work in spaces shared by many other people. That might sound silly, but think how many times a day you touch your phone with your hands and then bring the screen up to your ear!

In addition to singing in the appropriate range for your instrument, you want to speak at the proper pitch level for your voice. This is known as your *optimal pitch*. Nowadays, this is often higher than adolescents, and adult men habitually speak lower than adult women. If you ever have the opportunity to work with a speech therapist, do it. You typically spend many more hours a day speaking than singing, and positive speech habits will carry over into your singing.

Remember that to make any vocal sounds, including sneezing, laughing, crying, and especially shouting or yelling, you use your larynx ("voice box"), and that can potentially have a negative impact on your vocal folds. Obviously, the need for these sorts of vocal expressions will sometimes preclude vocal hygiene concerns, but when making these sounds in situations you can control, be smart in how you ration the use of your voice.

For example, in certain physical activities such as weightlifting, tennis, or self-defense, forceful grunting or yelling is encouraged. Also, performing certain theatrical roles will require loud crying or screaming, which can eventually hurt your voice. If you have to shout repeatedly because of the requirements of an acting role, the director may allow you to "mark" until you get to the final run-through. In this case, to "mark" means to hold back a bit on volume or intensity. Making that sound once or twice will cause a lot less wear and tear than doing it for hours on end.

Of course, you want to avoid unnecessary coughing/throat clearing whenever possible. Coughing brings the vocal folds together quite violently and can hurt your throat. Occasionally, this is habitual, but chronic coughing or throat clearing can often be an indication of an underlying problem that might require medical attention.

13. Medical considerations

Most singers would agree that seeing a doctor is a good idea if your voice is hoarse or raspy, especially if there are other symptoms present or a performance is coming up. Some other symptoms that you want to be on the lookout for include:

- Increased effort required to sing
- Dramatically reduced endurance (you can't sing anywhere near as long or as high/low as you used to)
- You can no longer sing softly
- Excessive mucus or a cold that never seems to go away

- Needing to use other muscle groups to "force" out sound

- Pain of any kind, particularly around the larynx

If you've never had a vocal injury, you might wonder what sorts of things doctors are looking for in vocal checkups. They want to make sure that your singing system looks and functions normally without signs of inflammation, such as redness, swelling, or the development of scar tissue. They also listen to your voice and will ask you how it feels to produce certain kinds of sounds. A good doctor will also ask about your general health and wellness; both physical and emotional stresses can have a very real impact on your voice.

You always want to make sure that you understand the vocal side effects of any drug you are prescribed, particularly if you receive that prescription from anyone other than a voice doctor. As a singer, your voice has special needs, and drugs that affect your hydration level, hormones, mucous amount, or thickness, etc. can have drastic effects on how your vocal folds work. You will probably notice these side effects far more than a non-singer. A wonderful database of common prescriptions is available on the website for the National Center for Voice and Speech www.ncvs.org/rx.html. Don't be shy about bringing this information to your doctor; he or she will often appreciate the help in picking out the most useful drug for your needs.

Similarly, you want to be careful with any medical procedures that involve a general anesthetic, as these generally require intubation (a small tube slid between your vocal folds). This is the kind of procedure that probably would have only nominal effects on a non-singer's speaking voice, but the singing voice is more sensitive. Talk to your anesthesiologist about using a smaller, "child-sized" tube, or a Laryngeal Mask Airway (LMA) for these types of procedures.

14. Your voice needs specialized care

Many people are unaware that their general practitioner does not actually see the vocal folds during a normal medical examination. Viewing and treating the vocal folds is a medical specialty. An *otolaryngologist* treats diseases of the ear, nose, and throat (ENT). ENT doctors have specialized equipment (including a laryngoscope, or "scope"), which allows them to see your vocal folds and surrounding areas.

However, many performers don't think of going to see a doctor when they are well, so the doctor doesn't have the opportunity to observe what the singing system looks and sounds like when they are in perfect health. If possible, a "baseline scope" is highly recommended. That way, any subsequent changes to your larynx or vocal folds can be monitored. If you plan to use your voice professionally, singers of all ages should have a good ENT physician on their medical team.

Sometimes, due to viruses or to overuse, obstructions can form on the edge of the vocal folds, like cysts and polyps. The word *nodule* (otherwise known as the dreaded vocal "*node*") refers to a callus on the vocal folds, somewhat like scar tissue on skin after a cut heals. The nodule prevents the vocal folds from completely coming together, resulting in a voice with an airy and/or raspy quality. The folds are often thickened as well, which makes it difficult or impossible to sing at your best. For these kinds of injuries, a course of treatment needs to be implemented by your ENT doctor, which might include voice rest, speech therapy, voice lessons, and medication.

A few tips from one of the top ENT doctors in the country, Gwen Korovin, M.D.:

Every vocal professional should try to establish a relationship with an otolaryngologist (ear, nose, and throat doctor) who specializes in the care of the voice. We are best known as laryngologists. Those of us who subspecialize in this area have a better understanding of the physical and emotional needs of performers than others in our generalized field. Someone who uses their voice partially or solely to make a living is really a vocal athlete, so treating these vocalists/athletes requires a vast amount of scientific knowledge and an expansive appreciation of the arts. Thus, it is a marriage of science and art.

A laryngologist may examine the vocal folds in a variety of ways. Sometimes a simple mirror exam is all that is necessary. Many physicians will skip this exam altogether, yet it is often sufficient and economical. If a patient needs a more extensive exam or has a strong gag reflex, a flexible laryngoscopy is performed. In this way, the nose, nasopharynx, oropharynx, hypopharynx, and larynx can all be seen, offering a better look at all the surrounding tissues. A rigid videostroboscopy provides a slow-motion exam with better light. The vocal fold edges and mobility are best visualized in this way. Still photos and videos can be made from these exams. A laryngologist usually has all of these instruments at their disposal.

Vocal professionals are often fearful about being seen by the doctor. They worry about discomfort or pain during the exams, but local anesthetics can be used if necessary. Skilled laryngologists are adept at performing these exams and can do them with great ease.

Dr. Gwen Korovin is an ENT-otolaryngologist in New York, New York and is affiliated with Lenox Hill Hospital. She has been called "Broadway's throat doc," and her patients have included too many luminaries to list, but include Celine Dion, Patti LuPone, Bruce Springsteen, Hugh Jackman, Julie Andrews, and Lady Gaga.

Chapter 3
Building Your Repertoire

15. What is your "book"?

Even when an audition provides specific music to be prepared, you might be asked to "bring your book." Every serious performer should have a collection of songs ready to be sung at a moment's notice. In our industry, your "book" is a physical binder that holds all of these songs, and is also the term for this repertoire of pieces that you have mastered and can perform with little or no preparation.

Your book is one of the few variables in the audition room that you have any real control over, so it is worth your time to put a great deal of love and care into its preparation and organization. You want every advantage walking into the audition room, so entering with a well-thought-out portfolio of your best work can be quite emotionally empowering. It also relays a lot of information about how seriously you take your work as an artist.

As they say, you don't get a second chance at to make a first impression. Just as in a job interview, the professional level of the materials you bring says a lot about you as a potential employee. Spend the time and the small amount of cash required to make it a great one!

16. Assembling your book

If you've ever been to a New York City open audition, you might have seen actors toting around giant binders of sheet music bursting at the seams with every song that they have ever learned. In addition to being cumbersome (probably weighing twenty pounds) and impossible to navigate quickly, these books often say more about the ego of the performer than they do to about how versatile a singer they are. As with everything, quality over quantity is the way to go. There are many singers out there that successfully use the same handful of songs over and over again at auditions because they know from experience that these are pieces they perform consistently well and are the most likely to achieve the principal goal: a callback.

Instead of one giant volume, I suggest that you start with three smaller binders: one for performance-ready pieces, one for works-in-progress, and one (or more) for storage. Your performance-ready binder that you bring to auditions should not be larger than one to two inches, and should be made of quality, durable materials; these are often marked "Heavy Duty" at office supply stores. D-type rings usually last longer than round ones. However, once pages start snagging on the edge, they need to be replaced. Your other binders can be larger, as you want them to house the remainder of your music library.

Having your music in a hard binder automatically presents it in a way that allows it to stand up firmly at the piano. I've played countless auditions where a singer brought in a handful of loose, photocopied pages and accidentally put them in the wrong order (because music books are larger than the 8.5 x 11 paper we photocopy music onto, things like page numbers are often cut off). Moreover, loose pages flying all over the room whenever an air conditioner turns on will certainly hinder your performance. Some actors will also opt for "accordion-style" taped pages, which I actually prefer to play from, but nowadays, 3-ring binders are the accepted industry norm. Remember, the easier you make it on the accompanist, who has probably been sight-reading inconsistently prepared music for hours on end, the better the music will sound, and the better your performance will be.

For some reason, the use of plastic sheet protectors to house your music is very controversial among Broadway accompanists. Some prefer matte or "non-glare" protectors, while others like the lightweight, transparent ones. I believe it doesn't matter what you use, as long as the pages are protected and easy to turn. Be careful when you sort your music that you only put pages from the same song back-to-back, so you don't accidentally remove the first or last page of a song whenever a piece moves from one binder to another.

You can skip the use of sheet protectors entirely if you copy your music double-sided on strong paper, and carefully hole-punch all your pages. You can also tape your pages side-by-side, or "accordion-style." Look at my website for an example of how to tape your sheet music in this fashion: www.bobmarks.com/info-tips/sheet-music.

Actors develop different systems for organizing music in their books. Some prefer to order by genre (Pre-Golden Age, Golden Age, Contemporary, etc.), while others might use an alphabetical system. Often, actors will use colored tabs from office supply stores to file their music into sub-categories, which can make music quite easy to locate in a pinch. Whichever you choose, you should be able to locate pieces immediately if a casting director asks you for another song you weren't expecting to perform that day.

17. Know genres and subgenres

When you first start digging into the vast array of musical theatre styles and genres out there, it can be pretty overwhelming. After all, you have about one hundred years of shows to catch up on! But with the help of the internet, it's easier than ever to immerse yourself in these classic musical scores. Broadway music is traditionally very self-referential, and directors expect working actors to understand basic tropes like the Act I "What do I want?" ballad or the eleven o'clock gospel number. Trust me; you don't want to be the only chorus member in *Urinetown* to miss that "Snuff that Girl" is an affectionate tribute to "Cool" in *West Side Story.*

There are three basic influences on how a show's music sounds:

1. the time period in which it was actually written

2. the time period of the show's plot

3. the year a production of the show is produced

If you listen carefully, there is almost always evidence of all three of these factors evident in musical scores. Nowadays, for example, it's common that revivals of legitimate, Golden Age musicals (shows originally produced on Broadway between the 1940s-1960s) are sung in slightly lower keys and with a more mixed registration to better match the vocal sounds of today. Also, because of improvements in wireless microphones, singers no longer have to work as hard to be heard over the orchestra.

As a guideline, the time period of an audition song is generally determined by its style, not the date it was actually written. For example, *Thoroughly Modern Millie* and *The Drowsy Chaperone* were both written in the 21st century, but feature scores that sound like they came straight out of the 1920s. In the majority of cases, you can use these pieces to audition for shows from the period they represent based on stylistic factors.

However, you really want to be careful that you understand those styles fully. There are songs in Andrew Lippa's *The Wild Party* that sound just like they are from the 1920s, but others that sound much like the year 2000, the year the show was produced off-Broadway. It all depends on the specific song that you choose and the requirements of the audition.

At present, casting calls for certain musicals (shows like *School of Rock* and *Rent* come to mind) specifically ask for "non-Broadway" songs. Depending on the style of the show, you'll want to look into material sung by pop performers who have a vocal range and style similar to the requirements of the show. The possibilities are endless, and it has become more and more important for the singer to develop a sense of appropriate style in addition to learning healthy technique.

18. Choose your first song

I think some actors really believe that there is one song out there that will get them all the work they could possibly want, and if they could only find that song, they would achieve all the success they desire.

Unfortunately, that is not the case. While your choice of audition song is an important consideration, I've never seen anyone get a part solely because they picked the right song. However, much like deciding what clothing to wear, song choice can work for you or against you. I'll admit it would be nice if there were a secret, foolproof set of guidelines out there you could use to pick songs that would always guarantee you a callback (and I would *definitely* sell more books if I could pass that formula on to you). However, the process of picking out an effective song involves several different factors and requires a bit of trial and error.

When you go shopping for nice evening wear, you probably spend a good amount of time trying on many different options. This can be either a fun or exasperating process, depending on how you look at it. Then, eventually, you try on that piece, which is the right fabric, style, and shape for you, and think, "this is the one!" When you get a piece of clothing like that off the rack and then proceed to get it tailored to your exact measurements, you will look and probably feel like a million bucks.

Similarly, to find a song that will highlight your best qualities, you will need to do a bit of legwork and will likely need to try out a few different options. The main goal of your song should be to show you off to your best advantage, so your age, type, vocal range, and the musical style of the show you're auditioning for must be considered. You can do this on your own, but a good coach who is familiar with a vast amount of repertoire, as well as your voice, personality, and look, will be able to save you a lot of time and trouble by helping you find song options that highlight your best qualities.

Don't be afraid to pursue a new spin on familiar songs in your coaching sessions; many casting directors love hearing risks that work. Sometimes a changed key or a fresh accompaniment is all that is needed to modify a song, so it fits you like a glove and doing an unusual selection for your type may emphasize something unique about you as a performer, such as flair for ironic humor. However, you want to make sure these are deliberate changes because some songs are considered to be rather sacred in the context of the show. Be careful to exercise good taste, and always do your research!

19. Find music that suits you

Just as you would build a wardrobe with varied outfits for different occasions and temperatures, your music repertoire book needs to feature a diverse selection of pieces to show you can handle different sorts of singing demands. Not every song can (or should) be a showstopper, full of dramatic heft and long, sustained high notes at the top of your range. Sometimes, it's more important to demonstrate naturalness and vulnerability or show that you understand the needs of a specific musical style. It's valuable to have many different kinds of songs in your "toolbox" to exhibit the full scope of your strengths.

A few decades ago, when music publishers were primarily editing musical theatre books for the enjoyment of amateur pianists, singers would need to search high and low to find sheet music that had even a passing resemblance to what was in the original show. Nowadays, editors have learned that singers want original versions of theatre songs, and there are some helpful commercial collections available. *The Singer's Musical Theatre Anthology* collection, published by Hal Leonard and edited by Richard Walters, has become something of an industry standard. These handy volumes are excerpted from the original vocal scores and are easy to find online or in bookstores categorized by voice type. Just one of these books will probably give you several months or years' worth of new repertoire to experiment with.

While you are hunting for new material, you should always be on the lookout for new possibilities. Attend classes, workshops, and seminars where you can hear songs that others are singing. Keep notes, and constantly ask yourself (especially with singers in your own age range and of similar "types") if the song is a good fit for the singer, and what effect the song has on you as the listener. Hearing other singers is also a great way to know if a song is currently overdone.

A word about finding material to sing on YouTube; as in all areas of your development, the key is to exercise common sense and discretion. Unfortunately, the vast amount of audio and visual material available on the internet has become a mixed blessing. Posted videos can be an illuminating but confusing place for source material. Students often want to imitate a certain singer or performance they've seen online, but when that performance is musically unfit or technically unsound, it can do more harm than good to rely on that performance as a teaching tool.

I like to remind my students that *anyone* can post a video, and just because they saw something online doesn't make it correct. However, sites like Vimeo and YouTube, as well as streaming services like Spotify, allow you access to many different recordings of songs and cast recordings. I would recommend that you listen to as many different versions of new pieces as you can to inspire you and help you brainstorm your own original "take" on a piece.

20. Examine the lyrics

Have you ever heard the expression, "nice house, nobody home?" Often, we use that phrase as a way to describe singers who make pretty sounds but fail to capture our imagination on the stage. It's an exceedingly rare performer who can communicate to an audience and make them feel something. Still, it is also the most essential quality a performer can possess in this business.

With a new song in hand, I know it's very tempting to jump in singing both the lyrics and music simultaneously. However, I suggest that you start by studying the lyrics separately from the music. Although it might take a bit of discipline, this indispensable step allows you to discover important truths about the character you are taking on. In this process, you will learn that the ideas and discoveries you glean from the words alone are essential to connect with your audience in an authentic, sincere, and organic fashion.

You must know the literal meaning of every single word of the lyrics, otherwise known as what the words are discussing on an "explicit" level. This allows you to know the realities of the character's situation, such as:

1. What has just happened to propel you into song?

2. To whom are you singing?

3. What is your relationship with that person?

4. What reactions are you getting to your words?

Don't hesitate to look up unfamiliar words, because you must know the meaning of every word you sing. This is especially important with words from a foreign language, idioms, expressions, historical and artistic references, etc. that are written into the lyrics. Try to immerse yourself in the text, and endeavor to have first-hand knowledge of every reference as if the words came from your own diary.

At this stage, you might ask yourself if communicating the written text truthfully requires experiences that you have not or could not have had yet in your life. For example, a child should probably not sing a song about the experience of having aged past her glorious prime, like in the song "Memory" from *Cats*. However, a song bursting with curiosity about what it might be like to fall in love for the first time, like "It Might as Well Be Spring," might be very appropriate for a tween or teenager to perform.

Finally, you want to examine the lyrics at an "implicit" level, which involves exploring what actors call "subtext"–the murky feelings that reside below the text, and may or may not be fully known to the character (there are some instances in which the actor needs to know more than the character does). Although we are often physically alone on stage and are almost always singing solo in audition situations, musical theatre songs always define a specific kind of relationship on both an explicit and an implicit level. Is the other person in the scene or the subject of the song your best friend that you've known for thirty years, or a new acquaintance that intimidates you? Both are "friends," which is the explicit relationship, but you can see how examining the "implicit" truth can paint a much more interesting story.

At all stages of the process, ask yourself, "Do these words make sense coming out of *my* mouth?" Don't get too frustrated if the answer is "no," and you are sent back to the drawing board a few times. Continued close examination of new material will help you to know yourself better as a singer and help you to determine what types of songs are relevant to your current life. Think of the "Hot/Cold" game we all played as kids; misses can be just as productive as hits if they help you pivot in the right direction.

I am frequently asked if, in an audition situation, you are bound by the original context and circumstances the song came from. I advise that, for the most part, you are free to create your own meanings and situations that suit you. The exception is that, if you're auditioning for a specific role in a show and are asked to sing that character's song, you should portray that character.

For the most part, I find it very handy to have students think of all songs as being somewhat autobiographical. The auditors are interested in your unique experiences and insights, which should be at the core of your connection to a new song. Just continue to use good judgment. If you are true to yourself, you will probably be the first to know if you are singing an inappropriate selection, or working on a piece that belongs in the "storage" binder for the time being.

21. Study each specific style carefully

Once you know your genres and sub-genres, you need to begin examining the nuances of each more carefully. As you add songs to your repertoire, make sure that you include contrasting pieces from the various genres of musical theatre. Where and when a show takes place often influences musical style, but the year a show was composed often reflects the singing styles of that period, so it's helpful to know when your song was written.

Here are some musical theatre styles worth exploring that might be missing from your current book:

Operetta: The Gilbert and Sullivan operettas of the early 20th century remain perennial favorites for many performance organizations, and not just because they're now in the public domain. These arias and ariettas are fertile ground for young romantic leads and character actors alike and give you a great chance to display your classical vocal technique. You might also want to look into operettas by Victor Herbert and Sigmund Romberg, as well as early Jerome Kern songs.

Pre-Golden Age/Jazz Age: Regrettably, these songs are rarely sung today, but musical comedy scores from the 1920s, 30s, and 40s are treasure troves full of some of the funniest and most sentimental music ever composed. Check out songwriters like Richard Rodgers and Lorenz Hart, George Gershwin, Irving Berlin, Cole Porter, and Kurt Weill. And you can't go wrong by adding a song by composer

Harold Arlen to your repertoire. He wrote many more gorgeous songs besides "Over the Rainbow." Look him up – you'll thank me.

Golden Age: Traditionally, this term is used to describe the classic book musicals from *Oklahoma!* (1943) to the Broadway opening of *Hair* (1968). This includes many of the great scores by Rodgers and Hammerstein, Lerner and Loewe, Comden and Green, Frank Loesser, Bock and Harnick, Jerry Herman, and Meredith Willson. At the time, before wireless body microphones, Broadway singers had to be loud enough to be heard over the orchestra. Leading ladies were usually either classical-sounding sopranos (like Barbara Cook) or loud belters (such as Ethel Merman). Leading men were often legit baritones such as Alfred Drake and Richard Kiley, and, back then, there were usually "character" roles that didn't always require a great singing voice.

Early Contemporary: Like everything else in the 1960s, the musical culture changed dramatically, so by the end of the decade, Broadway musicals were beginning to sound more like the popular music played on the radio. The increased presence of pop and rock began to reshape the audience's expectations of Broadway shows. By the 1970s, what used to be considered experimental was now normal. The "concept" shows of Stephen Sondheim began working their way into the literature, and even shows that seemed traditional, such as *Follies,* were not the romantic, feel-good shows of the Golden Age.

Modern: Around the 1980s, most new musicals began to be written with a contemporary/pop edge, and the British "megamusicals" like *Phantom of the Opera* and *Les Misérables* came to dominate the Broadway scene. As musicals became increasingly expensive to produce, large corporations like Disney began to become more and more involved. Although these experiments often were driven by economic incentives, they proved that, as long as producers focused on the artistic value of their project, huge conglomerates could create great theatre (*The Lion King,* for example).

2000 and Beyond: It seems that Broadway is once again undergoing something of a transition. On the one hand, we've enjoyed some great revivals of classic works. On the other, we are beginning to see scores emerge, embracing the experiences of traditionally underrepresented people like Asian-Americans and Hispanic-Americans. One of the exciting things about the musical theatre genre is that musicals can range stylistically from Latin rhythm and blues (*In the Heights*) to Afrobeat (*Fela!*) to hip-hop and rap (*Hamilton*).

Other selections in your repertoire book can include any styles that demonstrate your specific strengths, including opera, gospel, or jazz. As Cole Porter wrote, "Anything Goes!"

22. Research songs and shows

Recently, I had a sixteen-year-old client come in for a coaching session to prepare an audition for a television pilot. She would be playing a teenager who dreams of becoming a professional singer. She had been sent dialogue and a song to learn, but since she didn't read music, she needed my help. She assumed what they sent was an original song written for the show. As it turned out, it was "The Man That Got Away," probably one of the most famous songs ever written for the movies. Another time, an actor called me and said that her agent was sending her to audition for a show, and she needed to learn a "Cold Water" song very quickly. I thought for a second and asked her, "Did you mean Cole Porter?"

These anecdotes are humorous, but those are the kind of mistakes that may lead a professional to wonder how much you know about this business. The musical theatre community is small, so when auditioning for a show, it's best to appear to be a knowledgeable member of that community. Regardless of what you choose to sing, at the minimum, know what show it's from, and who wrote it. You may be asked!

If you are working on songs for which there are resources available, such as cast recordings, I recommend that you make use of them. This is not so you can imitate the original artists, but to help create the foundation for creating your own interpretations. It's not unusual for songs to have been written with specific performers in mind, structured specifically around their vocal gifts and/or placed in keys that maximized the strongest parts of their voices. Similarly, a tempo might have been selected because doing a lyric at that particular speed suited the original actor's type of comic timing or might have been needed to underscore a particular bit of stage action or choreography. You want to study these recordings for these clues as to how the original performance became successful, or, better yet, for ideas on how you can improve from the original.

Certain performance choices are so successful that they become part of musical theatre canon. For example, most actors wouldn't sing "Shy" from *Once Upon a Mattress* without placing the song in a key where they can belt the lyrics, "I've always been SHY," because it's obvious in the context of the scene that those sentiments are sincere but ironic. Carol Burnett's original performance of this character "stuck" because it worked so well and has helped inspire other interpretations that use this device for comic effect.

Even in these cases, the choices are not mandatory. However, to create an equally sensational singing performance, you have to substitute something great for something equally great (or even better). If you're trying to re-invent the wheel, it can never hurt to be armed with as much information as possible.

23. First, learn music accurately

Once you've decided on a song to learn, begun exploring the text and subtext, and done some listening research, take the time to learn the pitches of the melody as they are written on the music. It takes a lot longer to "un-learn" wrong notes than to learn the right ones the first time. If you don't read music, you'll need to work with someone who does, so they can record the melody for you to practice. Whatever method you use, make sure to really learn the notes and rhythm of a song before thinking of changing them. There's usually a good reason they were written that way.

Also, be sure you know the difference between the piano accompaniment and the melody. When you work with a coach or accompanist, it is beneficial to have him or her record your songs twice: once with just the melody plunked out, and once with just the accompaniment (which often does not include the melody). Again, make sure you take the melody quite literally before making any changes or adding runs and riffs.

Some singers find it helpful to learn an instrument, often the piano or guitar, to help learn and rehearse new songs. Although it's great if you can afford to go to a coach every time you have to learn a new song, people starting off in this industry don't always have that luxury. Reading music, even a little, will help you feel much more confident as a singer, not to mention, it will help you make a much better impression in rehearsals if you can learn music quickly. It also doesn't hurt when you have a lot of callback music to learn in a short period of time!

As a side note, with the recent success of so many productions requiring actors to play musical instruments, it is in your best interest to keep playing that instrument you studied back in school. I've never heard an actor tell me they wished they hadn't wasted time becoming musically literate, and there are many working performers today who are very thankful they never stopped playing their scales.

24. Plot out your phrases

After mastering the pitches, you need to plan where you will take breaths during the song. Most singers understand they need to be at least somewhat concerned about breath management. For your voice to function at its best, you generally need to have a comfortable reserve of air at all times; no one wants to run out of air in the middle of a word!

However, this is only part of the reason to strategize where you breathe. I sometimes think inexperienced singers feel that they will get an award for going the longest time without inhaling! Unless breath placement is planned and practiced, the lyrics of a song are often communicated as one giant run-on sentence. In truth, you are more likely to have a successful performance if you take the number of breaths that allow for the most expressive phrasing, which normally coincide with punctuation, musical phrases, and pivotal changes in the character's thought process.

Singers do not always seem to realize how important the placement of breaths is to convey their character's thoughts and feelings. When audiences listen to you, they hear the pauses in between phrases as punctuation, regardless of whether commas, periods, question marks, or exclamation points are written in the lyrics. This is particularly important in verses, which contain new information for the listener, and in opening choruses when your audience is being introduced to the themes of the song.

This is yet another reason not to learn songs from cast recordings alone. Like all of the other factors we've discussed, the best places for you to breathe might be different from another performer's choices. Studying the score lets you know where the authors themselves thought the best breaths might be located, giving you invaluable hints towards developing your own successful interpretation. I suggest taking the time to physically indicate breath marks in pencil so you have a concrete reminder of your plan that can be adjusted as you go.

Once you have carefully worked out your phrasing, you need to memorize it like all other elements of a song. Even if you're a quick study, a song that is recently learned will not sound as natural or polished as one that has been honed over a period of time. When you sing theatre music, you should be creating the illusion that you're expressing thoughts you've thought of for the very first time. To perform your best, you need to take the time to explore the nuances of how you are going to approach a song and give it time to become part of you.

25. Arrange and mark your music with care

Songs are like clothing: fit can be as important as the quality of the item itself, and alterations can make all the difference. In musical language, these changes might include moving the key lower or higher (transposition), making alterations in the accompaniment, changing the tempo, or cutting and pasting different sections together within a song to create a more unified excerpt.

Remember that an important goal of vocal coaching is to help a student display his or her unique set of strengths while minimizing limitations. Your individuality is what makes you a unique commercial commodity, and you will go much further building upon your natural abilities than doing a glorified imitation of someone else.

Be prepared to take constructive criticism from those you trust. Maybe you would like to belt like Patti LuPone, but you're actually a lyric soprano who sings in an obvious head voice. Or possibly you're someone who used to possess a certain voice type that has changed, like an aging baritone who insists that he's the same soaring tenor he was a long time ago back in high school. Know what roles and songs you're realistically right for now, and what might be possible with a great deal of instruction and practice.

Unless you're singing a particular song for a role in a specific show (which should be clearly indicated in the audition notice), you can and should have the song transposed into your best key. Nowadays, there are ways to have these transpositions done online at a very modest cost on websites like www.musicnotes.com. However, when you have pieces prepared through these services, always have someone play it through for you before bringing it to an audition. Pianists have countless horror stories about impossible-to-play sheet music from various online sources. Many coaches can help you not only create new accompaniments for your song, but can also prepare digital manuscripts that are ultra-legible for a sight-reading accompanist.

Remember, *you* are the one who will be doing the singing, so don't be afraid to express your opinions about what keys you place your songs in and what arrangement you choose to sing. I suggest that you record yourself often so you can make an educated call, confident that those changes do help you to sound your best. It's not unusual for students to find listening to their own recordings difficult at first, but over time, you will get used to it! A combination of good coaching and frequent use of recording devices (like those included on the average smartphone) can help by letting you know how others hear your voice.

26. Be careful with pronunciation and diction choices

Often, performers spend so much time learning to speak clearly that they neglect to think about how their diction choices are informed by the dramatic world their characters inhabit. When you watch period TV shows, you might notice how an actor's speech changes not only from region to region, but also from generation to generation. Similarly, to create fully realized characters, you have to take into account factors like:

- How much schooling has this character had? Was the character taught to speak in a certain way? Is there a certain way the character has been taught to speak that the character is now rebelling against?

- Does the character speak or sing with an accent, or is he or she deliberately trying to change the accent their family speaks with?

- How well does the character understand word choices (e.g., is the character accidentally mispronouncing words without even realizing it?)

- How confidently does the character use his or her voice? Does the character want to be heard by others, or does the character deliberately "cover" their voice, so others don't hear?

- What is the age and overall health of the character?

Such authenticity may be the most critical element of a successful singing performance. Remember, beautiful singing is important, but in the theatre, it is only part of the picture. Characters singing on their deathbed cannot and should not sound the same as they would on the happiest day of their lives.

One area in which commercial music departs from classical traditions is the shaping of vowels. In classical and operatic traditions, finding the most resonant, beautiful vowel is paramount. However, in commercial and popular styles, realistic, speech-like delivery is often more critical.

You always need to articulate your choices clearly. When you sing, I should be able to tell the difference between "sequence" and "sequins," "wary" and "worry," and "mist" and "midst." Remember how I said to spend some time working with just the text at the beginning? This will prevent you from misunderstanding the words in the first place! And pay special attention to correct pronunciations in cases where rhyme schemes depend on them.

For example, when Stephen Sondheim wrote the lyrics to "Let Me Entertain You" for *Gypsy*, the last line ("We'll have a real good time") requires the word "we'll" to sound like "wheel" to rhyme with "real." If you pronounce the word any other way, the rhyme is gone! You'll find that the right diction and pronunciation choices are often very organically connected to the rhythm, pitches, and world of the song and will almost always feel right when you come upon them.

27. Age, race, and gender considerations

I should point out here that, generally, I don't believe in performance "rules," but there are some guidelines that I think are good to have in the back of your mind regarding the appropriateness of certain types of repertoire. Some songs were written for a specific physical type or require the performer to draw from a particular set of life experiences, and sometimes race and/or gender are significant. For example, the character of Joanne in *Company* is a wealthy, twice-divorced alcoholic. It makes truly little sense for a high school student to sing her famous diatribe against young bourgeois women in "The Ladies Who Lunch" because the lyrics of the song require the character to be of a particular age.

It can be a bit of a gamble to change the age, ethnicity, gender, or overall type of a scripted character. Bear in mind, though, this is a business where *calculated* risks do have a habit of paying off. No one ever wins a role just because they took a risk. This only happens because the risk taken somehow added a new layer to the original material or brought out a brilliant quality in the performer.

For example, let's consider gender changes. These are sometimes possible with relatively little effort, as words like "he" and "she" rhyme, and most pronouns are only one syllable. However, you still need to handle these with care. Although it's theoretically feasible for a male performer to sing "I Could Have Danced All Night," it probably won't work in his favor, but songs such as "If I Loved You" and "Almost Like Being In Love" are equally fine for both male and female singers. In fact, if you research the source material, you'll discover that both the leading man and leading lady sing both of these songs together as a duet.

If you take on a role with traditionally ironclad casting perimeters, such as Effie White in *Dreamgirls,* who is normally cast as a rather voluptuous African American actress in her twenties, you need to be somewhat prepared for many audiences not accepting your rendition if you are a rail-thin Caucasian actor. Some professionals might be so taken aback by such an outside-the-box performance that they assume you are doing a humorous rendition of the song! Doing your research into the background of the show, as well as looking at the vogue trends in the industry, will allow you to see which boundaries are worth pushing.

Finally, it bears mentioning certain casting norms change over time. A production of *1776* staged after the advent of 2015's *Hamilton* will be more likely to consider actors of color in the roles of the founding fathers because producers now have incontestable financial evidence that modern audiences can be receptive of this concept. Of course, to those inside the Broadway community, this isn't very surprising. Broadway shows have always had a way of anticipating progressive social trends. It is entirely possible that in another few generations, the industry will look quite different than it does today and be the better for it. Even with this in mind, fifty years from now, it will be equally important to remain abreast of current casting trends.

28. Know your "type"

Actor, singer, and dancer Rusty Riegelman told me this story:

"I was performing in a dinner theatre production of *Oklahoma!* playing the role of Ado Annie, when I learned that Harold Prince was coming into town to cast a production of *Evita*. I was excited to be seen for this hit musical, but was aware that there was no 'Ado Annie' type in *Evita*. I decided to sing the only other song I knew, Rodgers and Hart's "Where or When," which was way beyond my usual singing comfort zone. After I finished the song, Mr. Prince asked me if I had any other song prepared. Well, all I was ready to sing was my *Oklahoma!* solo, "I Cain't Say No," a comedic belt song. After I sang it, the legendary director looked at me and said, 'That was good, but please don't ever sing that other song again!'"

To compile a comprehensive repertoire that shows off all your best vocal assets is like the proverbial journey of a thousand miles; you need to begin with a single step. Rather than attempting to find the perfect version of twenty perfect songs on your first try, play the "Hot-Cold" game with every song, each time inching closer to pieces that suit your instrument.

It's also appropriate to use this technique to make modifications to the same song. For example, if a piece is a great fit for your age, personality, and physical type, but slightly too high or low for your vocal range, play with the song in a variety of keys until you find the one that is just right. There is a fine line between pieces featuring a wide enough vocal range to evoke excitement in audiences but comfortable enough to avoid unpleasant, strained sounds, so most pieces will require a bit of trial and error in this area.

As you get to know your voice, you will begin to discover which vocal and physical categories you best fit into. Below, I've listed some great classic repertoire for each to help you get started. This is not, by any means, an exhaustive list of songs, or even of casting types. These songs are simply a starting point and are meant to be examples of the various genres of songs that can prove to be solid gold in any performer's arsenal.

For Children

It is an absolute must that the subject matter of the lyric is age-appropriate, with melodies placed within the comfortable vocal range of the performer. Obvious classic choices include songs from *Oliver!, The Sound of Music, Annie, The Secret Garden, Matilda,* and *Billy Elliot.* Also, don't be afraid of digging into off-Broadway scores like *Ruthless!* and *The Prince and the Pauper.* When auditioning for professional productions of these shows, children are often required to sing a number from the show they're auditioning for. "Where is Love" and "Consider Yourself" (*Oliver!*), "My Favorite Things" (*The Sound of Music*), "Tomorrow" (*Annie*), "Round-Shouldered Man" and "The Girl I Mean to Be" (*The Secret Garden*) are serviceable staples in any child singer's repertoire.

You might also consider songs written for child characters that are traditionally sung by adult actors, like in *John or Jen, You're A Good Man, Charlie Brown, Big River,* and *Anne of Green Gables,* but be very careful that you've made necessary key adjustments to accommodate the needs of developing voices.

A word on repertoire for "tweens:" although our society may view these young people as early-onset teens, often an 11 or 12-year-old will still have the larynx of a child even after they start thinking, dressing, and talking like a teenager. As always, use the best of care with these changing voices and be equally wary of song choices that feature inappropriate subject matter. Compare how Jason Robert Brown's musical *13* handles middle school social struggles, as opposed to the slightly older characters in *Grease* and *Bye Bye Birdie.* They may only be a few years apart in age but are worlds apart in maturity!

Teens

Performers that play between 13 and 17 years old should not usually sing songs that rely on decades of experience or memories. "Love, I Hear" (*A Funny Thing Happened on the Way to the Forum*), "The Boy Next Door" (*Meet Me in St. Louis*), and "Out There" (*Barnum*) are types of songs that work well for this age group.

As teenaged students are beginning to experiment with their social, intellectual, and artistic identities, they will often try to sing pieces that they emotionally identify with but are not always a great fit for their current equipment. That, mixed with a certain degree of vocal instability (normal for this stage), can leave many students confused and frustrated. A good coach can help students find their vocal footing during this rather turbulent time.

Adults

Adults historically have tended to fall into four different casting categories: Singing leads, singing character roles, singing chorus ("singers who dance"), and dancing chorus ("dancers who sing"). These classifications were primarily useful in knowing what sort of professional auditions to go to, although in recent years, we have seen a much broader interpretation of these categories, and the question of "What auditions should I go to?" becomes increasingly complex.

I urge you to not obsess too much over this information and assure you that the industry will indicate your "type" for you! Constantly getting called back for Laurie or Curley in *Oklahoma!* or Julie or Billy in *Carousel*? Chances are casting directors view you as a leading woman or man. If you tend to see a lot of comic scripts, such as Will or Ado Annie in *Oklahoma!* or Carrie in *Carousel,* you are probably seen as a young character actor.

Singing roles in standard musical theatre repertoire are often composed with specific vocal ranges in mind. Again, the rules of how low a soprano or how high a bass is supposed to sing are not etched in stone. However, these categories can serve as guidelines so you know what types of vocal colors the composers were thinking of to help you find additional new repertoire that will effectively "click" with your instrument. Most of the time, these are grouped into the following six different categories listed here from highest to lowest:

Soprano: The highest vocal range, sopranos might do well with Golden Age songs such as "No Other Love" (*Me and Juliet),* "Out of My Dreams" (*Oklahoma*), "One More Kiss" (*Follies*), and "Is It Really Me" *(110 in the Shade),* or more contemporary selections, such as "Let Us Be Glad" (*Wicked),* or "Practically Perfect" *(Mary Poppins).*

Mezzo-Soprano/Belter (sometimes lumped together with "Alto"): Mezzo-Soprano/Alto selections include "Always True to You in My Fashion" (*Kiss Me, Kate*), "Look to the Rainbow" (*Finian's Rainbow*), "What Did I Have That I Don't Have?" (*On A Clear Day You Can See Forever*), and "The Music That Makes Me Dance" (*Funny Girl*).

Tenor: For the Tenor, "Being Alive" (*Company*), "Younger Than Springtime" (*South Pacific*), "Take the Moment" (*Do I Hear A Waltz?*), and "I Will Follow You" (*Milk and Honey*).

Baritone: Baritone singers might look into "Sorry-Grateful" (*Company*), "I Still See Eliza" (*Paint Your Wagon*), "Good Thing Going" (*Merrily We Roll Along*), and "Promises, Promises" (*Promises, Promises*).

Baritenor: At the beginning of the 21st century, the hybrid "baritenor" category sprang up, which refers to male singing roles that require a rich, full quality but who have to frequently sing belt pitches that might have been challenging for even a tenor a few decades ago. Tread with caution if you are a baritone learning these roles, as many of them are really for tenors. Remember what we said in Chapter Two about singing too high and too loud for longer than your voice type permits!

Bass: Featured bass roles are not common in musical theatre other than Caiaphas in *Jesus Christ Superstar* and Jim in *Show Boat* (of "Ol' Man River" fame). It's pretty rare to stumble upon a legitimate bass nowadays, so if you have those kinds of low notes, your repertoire should definitely include a piece that features them.

Try to think of knowing your vocal type as an important asset rather than a limitation. It can even help you find great new repertoire for your voice that you would never have considered. For example, if you have been told a number of times that your lyric soprano voice is highly reminiscent of a young Kelli O'Hara, you might look into what roles she has played over her career. Most likely, you'll discover a handful of roles that work well for a similar voice type, regardless of whether they were written with a lyrical singing style (like Anna in *The King and I*) or musical comedy mix-belter (Nellie in *South Pacific*). The Internet Broadway Database (www.IBDB.com) can be a surprisingly fun and informative way to search for repertoire.

29. Know – but don't feel limited by – your type

I once had a client, a young lady with a lot of ballet training, who came to me looking to start her career in musicals. She didn't look at all like a traditional dancer, and she was a very inexperienced singer. However, she ended up making her Broadway debut as a featured member of the *corps de ballet* in *Phantom of the Opera*. How? She was cast in the role of Meg, Christine's friend and confidante, a character designed to visually and vocally compliment her taller, leaner, exquisitely voiced friend in the duet they sing together.

The entertainment industry can be an unpredictable place. One notoriously murky area is the subject of "typing," where performers are initially judged by their physical attributes. Understanding this process can be helpful for you to get a sense of what roles for which you might prepare. For example, if you have an audition for a production of *Oklahoma!*, it's good to know if your overall look and performance personality leans more towards Laurie or Ado Annie. This knowledge will help you pick audition pieces that highlight your strengths and show your potential to play one part over another. Also, when you have to choose between different prospective auditions, knowing your type can help you spend the most time at calls where the casting team are most likely to want someone with your particular blend of gifts, experience, and skills.

It can, however, seem that producers can never quite decide if they are looking for a more obvious or less traditional choice when casting. There are many famous examples of actors who were the opposite of the creator's original concept for a role. Take, for example, the extraordinary Ben Vereen, who in the 1970s was an almost completely unknown young, charismatic, African American triple threat. However, thanks to director Bob Fosse's persistence, he was cast as the original Leading Player in *Pippin*, a role originally conceived for an aging, non-dancing, Caucasian actor. Of course, the mold was broken again when an African American female performer, Patina Miller, played this part to great acclaim in the 2013 revival. Both Vereen and Miller won Tony Awards for their respective performances, illustrating that audiences are perhaps more responsive to talent over type than they are often given credit for.

It's true that when casting roles in productions where the audience has an existing picture in their minds of what the role might be, such as a Broadway adaptation of a famous film or television show, producers tend to anticipate audience expectations by casting performers that remind them of the original actors. Remember, many of the folks in casting are in the "business" part of "show business" and are often going to go with the candidate who is the most likely to provide a return on backers' investments (i.e., make the largest amount of their audience share happy). Sometimes this means going with the most conservative choice, but sometimes it means going in a gutsier direction.

For the actor, spending a lot of time trying to determine which calls to go out for may be time better spent in the practice room and studio boning up on their skills. So turn out for everything you can! In a lot of instances, you simply cannot know what the producers and directors are looking for because *they* usually don't know themselves! This is why casting breakdowns tend to be infuriatingly vague. Regardless, I encourage you to consider these sorts of auditions to be potential windows of opportunity. The less specific the description, the more different types of performers that are likely to be considered, and the more likely your talent will be considered over your height, weight, gender, ethnicity, or any other variable outside of your control.

Generally, when a call for an audition goes out, it is accompanied by a "breakdown." These include qualities casting directors are looking for, such as age, vocal type, or special skills like gymnastics, or ability to play a specific musical instrument. My advice is to use breakdowns to pinpoint the types of skills a producer might need. If you have never taken a dance class in your life but have a fantastic singing voice, it probably makes more sense to spend your afternoon at a *Les Misérables* open call than at *A Chorus Line* or *Cats*. Worry more about the skills that are being asked for, such as the ability to "mix-belt a high G" or "dance *en pointe*," and let those making the tough decisions worry if you are the right type.

Also, remember that the very things that make you wrong for one role might make you right for another. At the beginning of your career, it may seem that all of the available roles are for fit, model-attractive ingénues, but you will ultimately have the most success by marketing what makes you *unique*. If you are naturally and irrepressibly funny, don't try to conceal the fact. Simply be the funniest "you" at the audition.

Whenever you have trouble believing this, make a list of your top five favorite Broadway performers of all time. Ask yourself how many of the names you see became famous for imitating a more marketable "type," as opposed to applying their energies to becoming a unique and memorable powerhouse performer.

Even if one job doesn't pan out, it doesn't mean something else might not come out of an audition. When my student Lauren Conley auditioned for the Broadway company of *Matilda*, she quickly realized her dancing wasn't up to the requirements of the show. But when the casting people heard her incredible singing voice, it led to an audition for the Broadway revival of *Annie*.

30. Know when a new piece is ready

It's not uncommon to find yourself with only a few days (or even a few hours) to prepare for an important singing audition. At that point, it's probably too late to start trying to learn a new song, but impeccable and on-going preparation is the key to ensure that you will have the chance to showcase your skill and talent appropriately, regardless of what last-minute challenges or curveballs are thrown at you.

Although I rarely advocate for hard and fast unbreakable rules that guide what makes an audition successful, I would caution any singer against learning a brand-new song for an audition unless required. The ease of performing a song you know backward and forward is worth far more than the stress induced by performing a song–no matter how much you love it–before it's ready.

As long as it's in the general ballpark stylistically speaking, *how* you sing the song will almost always be more critical than *what* you sing. You can present a brilliant song choice, cleverly selected, and in the exact genre of the show in question. Still, if you are constantly distracted by a looming high note that terrifies you or a breath you can never quite remember to take, it's improbable that you will be at your best. You'll simply be too distracted to establish a strong dramatic focus. I have rarely encountered performers whose technique magically improves under duress.

Broadway performer, actor, director, and choreographer Peggy Lee Brennan got into the original Broadway production of *Grease* even though she sang what most would consider to be the "wrong" song. She arrived at the audition without an appropriate 1950s-style song, but sang something she was very comfortable with, "It's You" from the 1930s-style musical *Dames at Sea*. They liked what they heard, she got a callback, and came prepared with a song more appropriate for the show.

Here are some indicators that a piece is ready to go:

- You know every musical component of the song backward and forward. Every note, every rest, every breath, every pronunciation is something you could perform even when nervous, or a little sick, when hungry, flustered, or even if the monitor knocks the casting director's coffee off the table.

- You have run the piece on at least one occasion with a new pianist (preferably one that is sight-reading), so you know how clearly your music is laid out and marked.

- You have established such clear imagery in your mind's eye that you can remain focused on the storytelling regardless of how many pencils are dropped, wrong notes are played, or scowls you see. After all, if you are focusing on your imaginary scene partner, you won't necessarily notice what's going on in the room at all.

- If you struggle with performance anxiety, make sure you have sung the piece in front of an audience that has a similar effect on you (makes your pulse race, your stomach queasy, your breaths slightly shallower, etc.). It's not uncommon for performers to feel much more nervous performing in front of specific friends or family than auditors, so seek out supportive friends or family that allow you to experience how well you perform the song in a stressful situation.

- You have begun to think of this song as an old friend that will help you through a challenging situation, which, let's face it, most auditions end up feeling like.

The truth is, you might not have incontestable proof that a piece is ready until you finally perform it. This is a great case for auditioning as much as you can. Performing a "work-in-progress" at a low-stakes audition will give you critical information to assess how well it works for you. Better still, try to perform pieces within the safety net of a master class or workshop before you audition with it, where you can receive all the same info (sometimes more) without a potential job being at stake.

Some advice from casting director Jen Rudin:

My best advice for auditions of all kinds, especially singing: BE PREPARED! Your audition is the chance to show off your competitive notes, so choose a song cut that shows your strong notes. Do NOT ever come to an audition with a song you have never sung before.

Also, I love to hear a song that's familiar. It's hard to judge your skills if the song is not well known!

Jen Rudin is an award-winning casting director and author of "Confessions of a Casting Director: Help Actors Land Any Role with Secrets from Inside the Audition Room." (Harper Collins/ It Books, 2013). Visit www.jenrudin.com and follow @RudinJen.

31. Your preparation checklist

If you have followed all of the suggestions in this book thus far, you are probably in a great place with a number of new pieces. Here is a list of suggestions to help you make the final leap from "renting" a piece to owning it outright. If a song you are working on doesn't measure up yet, simply file it in your "working" binder until it's ready to help you sound great.

- Learn the whole song. Even if you are only asked to sing 16 bars at auditions, it is in your best interest to know the entire piece from top to bottom, especially those verses that are rarely performed (you'll find that Pre-Golden Age songs frequently have these). It's embarrassing to not be able to sing the entire song if requested, and, if a director asks to hear more, it means that they are interested in what you have to offer. Why deny yourself such an advantage?

- Also, I think it's next to impossible to fully understand a song's full meaning without taking all available information into account. There might be a minor reveal in one of those obscure lyrics that completely alters the significance of the song for you, allowing your interpretation to have a unique, fresh perspective that other "skin-deep" renditions of the same piece might lack. Imagine how refreshing it would be if you were a casting director listening to dozens of actors sing the same piece, and then finally stumbled upon a performer who took such an approach. If you were that casting director, who would *you* call back?

- When singing a cut of a song, make sure the excerpt reflects a "whole" selection, and it presents as a story with a clear beginning, middle, and end. Don't ever just start from the top and sing until you are awkwardly cut off somewhere in the middle. Bear in mind that the climax of the song, which often correlates with the "money" note or the key character realization, is usually found somewhere in the final third of a song. Make sure you construct your cut around that portion!

- Know, without a moment's hesitation, to whom you are singing, what you are singing about, and the meaning of every single word of the lyrics. In other words, make sure to keep up the work you focused on back in key number 20. I often recommend placing your imaginary subject just above the eye level of the auditors. Use discretion when making eye contact with the folks behind the table as you sing. Some directors might find it engaging, but most find it off-putting.

- Know exactly what your character wants. Pretty much every song ever written has to do with a character wanting something and wanting that thing very, very badly. Perhaps they wish to be loved, to be heard, to be kissed, to be fed, or to be put out of their misery. Maybe they want revenge, forgiveness, a raise, a job, or a second piece of pie. Regardless of what it is, the only reason why you would start singing about it in the context of a musical is because you want that thing so desperately that speaking will simply no longer suffice. Make it clear what you want and make getting it the most important thing in the history of the world for that 45 to 90 seconds you get to sing.

- Allow the piece to start to take on a life of its own. There are few things more engaging to an audience than watching a well-versed performer continue to make new, performance-enhancing discoveries. If you are in a place where every time you sing a piece, a new "light bulb" turns on, adding layers of nuance and sophistication to your existing work, it is probably ready to make its debut.

32. Keep your book organized

If you have done all the hard work involved in preparing a piece of music thoroughly, it seems tragic to let a small detail like poorly photocopied music or mixed-up pages prevent you from getting a callback. This is somewhat like taking all the trouble to graduate top of your class at Harvard Law only to show up at your first major interview in ripped jeans and flip-flops. True, it's possible that a true genius might still be offered the job despite what he or she was wearing, but why on earth would you go through all that effort, only to then give yourself an avoidable handicap to overcome?

Keeping a well-organized book allows you to look and feel like a polished professional during the audition process. An impeccable book offers you an invaluable sense of control in how you present yourself, and gives those who are thinking about hiring you important clues regarding what sort of colleague you might turn out to be.

To illustrate this point, put yourself a casting director's shoes for a moment. Actor A comes in and rushes rather nervously to the piano, where he throws a few upside down, coffee-stained photocopies to the accompanist. He sings surprisingly well, despite the pianist missing key changes because the pages were out of order. He performs so well that the team would love to hear more, but sadly, Actor A left the rest of his book back in his apartment.

Compare his chances of landing the job to Actor B, who walks in the room with a neat, navigable book that the accompanist can negotiate easily. Although the Actors A and B are comparably talented singers, it's a little easier to focus on Actor B's nuanced acting performance without all of those wrong notes in the accompaniment. Since we see Actor B has a nice-sized book in tow, we ask him for a second song, and he can turn one page to get to it.

In Actor A's case, we can only assume that he is coming in with the only song he knows (despite what he may have said) and could not be bothered to have presented even that one song in a professional manner. In the case of Actor B, we will make the reasonable guess that this is one of many pieces the performer has carefully prepared, which also indicates to us that he or she will be able to handle things like learning lines and challenging music without any trouble on our part. In other words, although both actors might appear at the onset to have a similar level of vocal talent and charisma, Actor B presents as being far more *skilled*.

Now, if you had to stake your reputation on one of those actors, which would you choose?

Although it seems like a no-brainer, I am always amazed at how often singers will leave photocopies of cut-off music in their binders, or not bother to even look through their music once before handing it to the sight-reading pianist to make sure the pages are in the right order. True, sometimes this is because the actor cannot read music, but a very quick session with a coach or even a musical friend can make all the difference. Be honest with your abilities here, and don't be afraid to hire help if you need it. I sometimes wonder if young actors who are willing to spend countless hours waiting to be seen at an open audition but "don't have time" or "can't afford to" make a thirty-minute appointment to prepare in advance, secretly know they might be in the wrong line of work.

One final hint that bears repeating–if you use plastic sleeves in your book, make sure to arrange your music so the last page of one song is not the first page of another. You'll be amazed how often you'll accidentally take out both, and how easy it is not to notice until your casting director asks for that second song!

33. Increase your repertoire

Finally, it's time to start increasing your repertoire to include a greater variety of songs in different styles. We live in a golden age of musical diversity. Never before have Broadway scores featured a more eclectic array of songwriting styles – a commercial reality that you should take into account when crafting your book. However, consider this requirement a fun and gratifying challenge as you look for new, different, exciting pieces with which you have a personal affinity. Don't rule out any genres in which you excel; you never know if there will be a show opening next year looking for singers who are experts in that exact style.

In the meantime, it might be a good idea to start digging into industry job listings on www.backstage.com, www.playbill.com, or www.actorsaccess.com to get an idea of what types of songs are currently in special demand. For example, after *Rent* became a pop culture sensation in the 1990s, it became quite common for casting directors to specifically ask for songs from outside the traditional musical theatre repertoire. For many actors, this might have been the first time they thought to include other types of songs in their book since the 1970s! Nowadays, any given Broadway season features endless varieties of new and classic sub-genres. Keep honing your specific skills and the qualities that make your performance memorable and special.

Although it's never a bad time to start working with a coach, you might find this stage to be the perfect time to get a fresh perspective.

You might even consider seeing a brand-new coach for a trial session or taking an audition master class with an instructor who doesn't know your work. Someone who has never seen you or heard you before is going to give you the best sense of what judgments casting directors might make about you or your chosen material, and they might have some fascinating and helpful insights for you. Listen to their feedback carefully, and don't be afraid to ask for practical applications, such as what roles they suggest you look into, or if they think the songs you are using now are good for your type. Making a good first impression is the basis of auditioning.

Rather than thinking of their responses as restrictive or limiting, use the information they give you as a license to seek out roles you would never have considered for yourself. Besides, a good teacher will not frame this information as, "You're over six and a half feet tall and slender... it's ridiculous to think of playing a juvenile lead," but instead will say, "Lucky you! Because you have such a unique body type, here are some roles that you should look into that most of my clients can't play convincingly." Or, "Wow, when I was casting this show last month, I sure could have used more performers who look and sound like you!"

Happy hunting!

Chapter 4

Mastering the Art of Auditioning

34. Make a game plan for each audition

One of the most common mistakes that young performers make when preparing for auditions is overthinking their selection, especially when they're letting the pressure of the holding pen paralyze them with unnecessary self-doubt. Choose your piece in advance and trust that your homework has prepared you. It's always better to avoid making important decisions at auditions (and, probably, throughout life in general) when under the influence of adrenaline.

If you have not done the necessary work in advance, switching to a less familiar selection at the last minute will rarely work in your favor. Besides, if you make the wrong decision but are the right candidate for the role, the auditors will probably take a moment to work with you. Remember, their goal is to cast a show with the best available talent; if they see a great contender for a role, they won't let her slip through their fingers without giving her a fair shake. However, if you choose to sing a piece you barely know because you just heard someone sing "your song" a few minutes before, there is very little chance that they will be able to evaluate your potential fairly.

Sometimes you will be in a situation where you really cannot decide what to sing because you don't have enough information. Perhaps it's because you're auditioning for a new musical and have no idea on what types of material your character would be asked to do beyond "contemporary" or "classical," or the production team has just announced that they are looking for non-traditional choices for roles that would normally be considered to be outside of your type. In this case, I suggest offering two contrasting choices, then ask the auditors to choose. However, be prepared for them to turn the question back on you, or say, "Sing whichever is your favorite," in which case, have a plan prior to walking in the room of which one you'll do.

It will be in your best interest to practice several different contingency plans for less-than-ideal situations. This is one area in which I think you might benefit from listening to audition horror stories from your peers–it will give you ideas about what sorts of distractions you can prepare for. It's entirely possible that you might be asked to sing an accompanied piece *a cappella* (without accompaniment), sing with a track when you thought there would be a live accompanist (or vice versa), or sing much less or more than was instructed in the job posting. It's also possible that any number of disruptive sounds, like a cell phone or a heating vent, might suddenly blast through the air at the worst possible moment. An accompanist's reading glasses could fall off, causing the music to suddenly stop, or the choreographer might even spill a bottle of water all over the floor. Being as prepared as possible may make the difference between a successful audition experience and one that you'll want to forget!

Kathy Morath, Broadway performer, director, and educator told me about one of her memorable audition experiences:

A blizzard is raging on a frigid January morning but my final callback for the leading lady in The Goodspeed Opera's production of *One Touch of Venus* is still on. The audition is being held at the old King Studios on 42nd Street and 12th Avenue, a long walk from the IRT subway stop in Times Square. But I've vocalized, my hair is in an up-do and I'm dressed in a gorgeous winter white suit. I have my thermos of hot tea, sheet music and sides, and of course my smart Kenneth Cole beige pumps to finish off my look.

Since about six inches of snow is already on the ground and it's still coming down, I'm wearing my sturdy if clunky knee-high L.L. Bean Duck Boots with faux fur lining. These boots are keeping my feet, ankles, and shins warm and toasty. I'm such a clever girl! I arrive at the studio, shake off the snow, fluff out my hair, then reach into my tote bag for my pumps. NO PUMPS!!! The monitor whispers to me, "You're lucky, we're running early. You'll be next!" No time to dash home.

With only two options available to me, I am on the horns of a dilemma: Do I pad into the audition room in my stocking feet (I was wearing pantyhose) or do I lumber into the room in my dorky L.L. Bean Duck Boots?

I went with the boots.

So, I marched right into the room (making no apologies and giving no explanations) and the table fell apart with laughter. I was embarrassed but I forged ahead with my audition. I sang my heart out, read scenes from the script, took adjustments from the Musical Director and the Director, then politely thanked the team. The Director came bounding out from behind the table to shake my hand. They liked me!

It was weeks later that I found out that the entire creative team had assumed that my wearing those boots was a conscious wardrobe decision I had made to echo the character's sense of being in two worlds at once, and of remaining the proverbial "fish out of water." What I had perceived as an epic fail was actually a blessing in disguise. And my "mistake" taught me an important lesson – two actually. The first is, "Work With What You've Got" and the second, "Never Complain, Never Explain."

Today I pass this wisdom on to all of my students. And, guess what? The Kenneth Cole pumps are long gone, but I still own those L.L. Bean Duck Boots.

35. Keep track of your auditions

If you are still a student or are new to the business, it might be hard to imagine that there will be a time very soon when you will have attended so many auditions that you'll have difficulty keeping them straight in your mind. When actors are between jobs, the number of auditions they attend quickly adds up. When you start to get callbacks, it's entirely possible that you may have trouble remembering exactly which combination of factors was so successful in getting you through the door.

If a casting director calls you back in, it is likely because you were perceived as being a candidate who could fulfill the exact needs of a role *as you came in* on the day of your audition. If you show up to your callback wearing a sexy short dress rather than the floral peasant skirt they remember, or with a "Grizzly Adams" beard instead of the clean, groomed goatee you auditioned with, you might appear an altogether different performer.

I suggest keeping a written log, perhaps even an Excel spreadsheet, of which auditions you attended, including as much of the following info:

- The name of the show
- The date and location of the audition
- What piece(s) you sang
- What you wore/your hairstyle
- Any info you have about what individuals might have been behind the table (directors, producers, casting associates, etc.)

As a side note, it's also assumed that you will look like the person whose headshot was submitted. Some performers use a variety of pictures to capture different perspectives of their performance personality; for example, if they have both a "comic" and "dramatic" body of work. If this is the case, you might want to keep track of which picture you sent in, so if you're called for an appointment, you don't leave the auditors asking, "Who is this person?"

36. For each audition, know as much about the show as possible

There are lots of advantages to living in the information age, where all manner of media is instantly available at your fingertips. However, for the novice performer, there is one rather notable downside to such unlimited access.

Because virtually every cast album ever recorded is available to stream somewhere on the internet and every show open even briefly on Broadway has been documented faithfully on musical theatre history sites and blogs, you are no longer permitted to plead ignorance when it comes to research. Unless the musical for which you are auditioning is brand new or exceedingly obscure, the general expectation at professional auditions is that you have done some or all of the following: listened to all available cast recordings, watched any available videos, read a detailed synopsis of the show, and, if commercially available, read the script itself. It's true that, in some situations, you won't have the time to do this sort of leg work, but whenever possible, make sure to expand your preparation beyond the one or two-sentence breakdowns on the casting call.

The further you go into callbacks, the more important this legwork becomes. Asking a director what exactly Maria did to upset Anita or why Jean Valjean ended up in prison in the first place will not win you many points with creative teams, and you might elicit accidental snickers – not the impression you want to make when looking for a gig. Remember how we stressed professionally formatting your book to highlight your experience and abilities? Regardless of how well you sing, demonstrating gaping holes in your knowledge of the musical theatre canon can leave directors questioning whether you have an adequate understanding of the art form.

Now, to be clear, auditions are not academic research papers, and you are not expected to cite formal, scholarly sources when doing show research. Common sense will probably tell you in a few sentences of reading if the source you are looking at is adequately reputable for your purposes or not. You'll find, for example, because only musical theatre aficionados seem to do the updating, sites like Wikipedia are a perfectly reliable place to start researching the production histories of musicals and often provide a great works cited section if you want to examine the sources more closely. Better still, when you are preparing, make sure you have exhausted sources available to you through YouTube, Spotify, Apple Music, Google, or even the scripts, scores, and CDs available through your local library.

37. Be informed about every selection you sing

I will keep this one short and sweet, as it doesn't require much elaboration.

Know who wrote the song you're singing, how to pronounce their names, what show it's from, and what character sings it. You will be asked more often than you expect, and you will be very, very embarrassed if you don't know.

38. Know what a "bar" really is

One of the most common misconceptions I find myself needing to address over and over again is the myth that "16-bar cuts" should always be 16 literal bars of music. Limiting an audition to 16 bars is an issue of time, but a musical bar is *not* a quantity of time, which admittedly is a very confusing distinction.

If you are a novice music reader, a "bar" or a "measure" means one unit of music, which is segmented by two vertical lines. They act as rhythmic signposts and appear after a certain number of predetermined rhythmic intervals, usually after two, three, or four beats. Think about when you take a ballroom dance class, and the teacher counts out "ONE-two-three, ONE-two-three" when you dance a waltz, or "ONE-and-two-and, ONE-and two-and" when you dance a bright two-step. Each time they go back to "one," that would indicate the beginning of a new measure in your sheet.

You might wonder, then, how 16 bars of a song with two fast beats per measure (such as a fast march, like "Yankee Doodle Dandy") and a slow ballad with four long beats per measure (think "Send in The Clowns" or "Memory") could be the same length. The truth is, they are not! A bar of "Yankee Doodle Dandy" will be about one second long, while each bar of "Send in the Clowns" will probably take five or six seconds to perform. Pretty big difference!

I've always felt that requesting 16 bars of a singer's repertoire is somewhat unfair. It's like asking someone to bring 16 pieces of fruit to a picnic; 16 grapes are vastly different than 16 watermelons. However, since this is the common industry norm, let's talk about what is generally expected when auditors ask for "32," "16," and "8" bar cuts.

Generally, I assume a bar to be about two seconds in duration. At that rate, a 16-bar song would last about 32 seconds; allowing for a short introduction and an extended ending, I advise my students to cut 16-bar selections to under a minute, preferably around 45 seconds. Sometimes in a really big cattle call, producers will only ask for an 8-bar cut, in which case you would likely do the second half of a 16-bar cut (roughly 20-25 seconds). A 32-bar selection should also be measured by time, ideally no more than 90 seconds of music.

The beauty of this guideline is that it is very easy to follow. If you're not sure how long your cut is, just pull out the stopwatch on your phone and sing it through (making sure to hum through the intro, as well). If you are nervous about whether the pianist will refuse to play your well-crafted 17 or 15-bar excerpt, remember that the whole reason auditors ask for cuts in the first place is to save time. It will take more time to count the exact number of bars and communicate to you the cut is too long than to just let you sing them. As long as you are in the right ballpark, you should be in great shape!

39. Understand the requirements of good 16-bar cuts

At this point, you might be wondering why so many auditions require that singers prepare 16 bars of an audition song if the exact number of bars is effectively meaningless. Also, if this instruction is not to be followed verbatim, what exactly are auditors looking for with this directive?

For our answer, we have to go back to the earlier days of musical theatre. In the pre-pop days of musical theatre, when the standard American song was the same 32 bars repeated for the number of verses written (usually in AABA form), to ask for a 16-bar cut was simply the fastest and simplest way to explain to the singer just to sing the bridge ("B" section) leading into the final "A" section. This was and remains, a pretty straightforward formula and is often still perfectly acceptable for many selections that use this relatively common song form.

However, nowadays, Broadway songs use many more creative "recipes" in their song structure and creating a good 16-bar selection does not always just mean counting 16 bars backward from the end. Often, you will need to experiment with several sections of a song or even combine different sections. Some of the features of a good 16-bar audition cut will include all or most of the following:

- It should sound like an entire piece, only shorter, and have a logical resolution, harmonically (in other words, should end on a "conclusive sounding" chord), and dramatically. Rhythmically, there will often be a "button," like a last bass note or a final high chord in the accompaniment, to let the listener know the selection is definitively finished.

- Even if different sections are artfully stitched together, they must maintain the integrity of the music. In other words, if someone has never heard the song before, they should feel as if they are listening to an uncut version.

- The piece must be playable at sight by an unfamiliar accompanist (more on this later).

- The piece must show off the vocal strengths of the performer; often, this will include the highest and/or lowest notes you can sing consistently in the style of the show.

- The cut must make a coherent dramatic statement and have a clear narrative arc. Even if the scope of the story you are telling is much smaller than it might be in the context of the show, it should still have a feeling of "Once upon a time… then this happened… which changed me from this type of person to this type of person… the end."

- The text should reflect a complete story. Avoid beginning cuts with words such as "but" or "and." Listeners should not feel that they have missed something.

- If the cut of your song changes keys, consider the musical transitions when making a cut.

This cut MUST be prepared in advance. A singer should never go into an audition unsure of exactly what to sing and what the accompanist is expected to play. It is a rookie mistake to start from the beginning of the song and expect to be cut off. First of all, if an audition piece goes on too long, it may appear that the singer did not follow the instructions. Also, as I'll address in a moment, in the audition room, longer is not usually better. Your goal is to leave them wanting *more*, ultimately resulting in a callback!

With my students, I often start the process by deciding which part of the song best shows off "money notes" or the memorable "show-off" notes in the singer's range, which are often found at or near the end of the piece.

If the song is to be played at a moderate tempo, another common method is to count 16 measures back from the beginning of the last note, not including the "ride out," or the music that is played under the final syllable of the lyric, and may be as short as one note, or as long as several measures.

However, at times, one might find that the first 8 bars plus the final 8 bars make a better arrangement. Sometimes, the music from one section makes more sense with lyrics from a different section. Many contemporary music theatre songs are quite lengthy, with multiple changes of tempo, style, and range in one piece (think of how many are visited in Jeanine Tesori's stylistic showcase, "The Girl in 14G"). When dealing with this type of music, there may be several 16-bar possibilities, all of them valid. There is not one specific, foolproof method; just try different versions that protect the rhyme scheme, maintain the logic of the storytelling, and retain a cohesive musical line.

Remember that the principal function of 16-bar or 8-bar cuts are essentially typecasting to determine whether you will go on to the next step of the audition process. Although appearance or physical type counts as much as anything else, since the panel is seeing and hearing the performer for the first time, it is important to demonstrate more than just an appealing voice. Performers need to communicate who they are and show their strengths as actors and singers.

Since this initial evaluation rarely, if ever, results in a job, there is only one possible positive result: a callback in which more time is allowed for detailed appraisal. The initial 16-bar audition must generate the auditor's interest enough that the performer's picture and resume gets placed on the callback pile instead of in the garbage can.

Maureen Mershon, who has spent most of her life in the theatre as a performer, director, and teacher, recounted a memorable audition she had at the Actors' Equity offices. She signed up for an open call at dawn, but wasn't seen until many hours later, at dusk. When she finally got in the audition room, she was asked to sing only four bars! She told me, "Thankfully, I always knew where my money notes were, and sang the last three lyrics of 'I Don't Care' in my biggest belt voice, and stayed within four bars. I got the job!"

40. Understand the requirements of 32-bar cuts

For a 32-bar cut, all of the same considerations apply regarding the dramatic arc of the piece, harmonic resolution, etc. Remember that because you are not doubling the intro and outro, a 32-bar selection should not quite be twice as long as a 16-bar cut. As a general guideline, try to keep the entire performance to 90 seconds long at the maximum.

41. Understand the requirements of full songs

In the rare and fortunate event that you are asked to sing an entire song, choose songs (or cuts of songs) that are no longer than two minutes in length. As I've said earlier, longer is not better, and if you haven't impressed them in the first minute of your song, it's probably not going to happen in the second minute.

I sometimes compare audition songs to slices of pizza. Have you ever noticed how the first slice or two of pizza might taste delicious, but then every extra piece you eat is just "more?" Rather than giving the auditors multiple pieces of pizza during the audition by singing in the same range, the same key, the same melody, etc., take advantage of having more time and opportunity by giving them a whole buffet; appetizer, followed by the pizza, and topped off with an irresistible dessert. In other words, try to give them a performance that would have been impossible to deliver in only 16 bars of time. For example, you might find a song with a thrilling series of modulations, or that features an unexpected stylistic shift halfway through, showing off your versatility.

Whatever you do, don't just sing two choruses instead of one: make the extra time count! You'd be amazed how much of yourself can be showcased with some strategic decisions and a little elbow grease.

42. Specific audition situation: College admissions

I get a lot of questions about college auditions, and how they might differ from other sorts of acting or singing auditions. Contrary to what you might discern from college audition blogs or other online sources, I don't think it's possible to generalize qualities that *all* schools are looking for.

In the United States, performing arts schools come in all sizes and flavors, ranging from two-year certificate programs focused entirely on vocational performance skills (singing, acting, and dancing) to graduate programs centered on rigorous theatre scholarship. Because the work expected upon entrance is so school-specific, all of these schools are going to have different entrance criteria.

Most frustrating is that, because college websites and admissions offices are usually run by different people than those who conduct the auditions, it's possible that even great departments can do a pretty poor job at communicating their expectations to incoming students. What you must do first is pick which schools you'd like to audition for, then you can pick audition material that highlights why you would be a great candidate for their programs. Here are some quick tips on how to do this:

- When you're in the research stage, ask people who know you and know your work, especially teachers, coaches, and directors you've had, about schools that might be a good fit for you.

- Consider auditioning for at least a few different types of programs (state schools, private colleges, B.F.A. (Bachelor of Fine Arts) programs, B.A. (Bachelor of Arts) programs, etc.), so you can consider different options. You might be surprised at what kinds of campuses appeal to you.

- Make sure that you understand the academic criteria for acceptance, as well. Often, arts departments will decide on your acceptance before or after you've been admitted to the college or university itself. It's pretty common for students to be accepted into one but not the other.

- Although social media is a great place to enquire about campuses, take each endorsement or criticism with a grain of salt. However, if lots of people share the same impression of the program (especially those who know you personally), you might want to give those perspectives more weight.

- Sit in on as many classes and/or performances as you can. Although these are not always part of the school's "official tour," usually by calling or emailing faculty directly, you can ask for permission to visit. Just make sure to clear this in advance with the school, especially if you're asking to see something not ordinarily open to the public.

- Sometimes you can arrange to have a private lesson with one of the school's faculty voice teachers or coaches. Although there is no guarantee that you will end up with that teacher, you will glean valuable information about what sort of musical and dramatic values will be stressed in that department. You might get some pointers as to what sort of qualities they look for in prospective students.

- If at all possible, see a fully staged performance at the prospective school and, if possible, less formal performances such as workshops or recitals.

The bottom line for your selection should be: does the school teach the kinds of skills I want to learn? If it doesn't, don't waste your valuable time or money. Even if you get in with a full scholarship, you probably won't be happy there. Incidentally, lots of schools are happy to comp tickets for prospective students, so don't be afraid to let them know you're coming.

At the audition itself:

- Make sure that you follow the audition criteria that you are given to the absolute letter. If the directions say, "16 bars," in this one instance, make sure you have interpreted those directions quite literally. However, just like a regular audition, you might want to consider having a few contrasting backup selections with you in case you are asked.

- Remember that you are (hopefully) being listened to by seasoned educators who are not looking for "finished products" as much as they are looking for willing, dedicated practitioners who demonstrate strong potential. Resist the urge to focus on pleasing the auditors and trust they want to see your honest, current, and authentic self. Let your future professors hold the responsibility of looking decades into the future and projecting what your skills will look like on a character in his thirties or forties.

Finally, remember that schools are usually looking for students who appear to be the right fit for their particular program. A very intellectual student who is interested in a host of other subjects might not seem like the best fit for a competitive B.F.A. or conservatory program. Similarly, a student who wants desperately to sing, dance, and act every waking hour of the day and night might not seem like the best fit for a B.A. program that emphasizes a more broadly-based liberal arts curriculum.

Don't take first rejections (or acceptances, for that matter) to heart. Use them as a moment for reflection. Sometimes unexpected acceptances and rejections teach us things about ourselves we don't know yet. Assume the folks at the table are on your side and want the brightest possible future for you. They don't want to admit you to a program where they feel you won't succeed, and want to save you the time and expense of matriculating in a program that will derail you from achieving your goals.

Remember that, although many performers consider their alma mater the reason they've been so successful, countless performers have had wonderful performance careers without college. Also, the decision to attend or not attend school is hardly final; you always have the option of transferring, auditioning again, etc. Take the time to look at your goals and your abilities and see what makes the most sense for you *right now.*

43. Specific audition situation: "StrawHats"/Season auditions

Combined auditions can be a great way to be seen by many prospective casting directors at once, and some, like StrawHats, NETC (New England Theatre Conference), or SETC (Southeastern Theatre Conference) can be a particularly wise move at the beginning of your career. True, many of the available jobs may be for fairly low-paying ensemble roles. Still, for young or developing performers, these auditions provide a great opportunity to gain valuable professional credits. Also, many of these companies are casting with a full season in mind, so one audition might ultimately yield a contract for a half-dozen different shows.

The downside is that you will have little time to make an impression. Many of the regional auditions ask for less than two minutes of material for a monologue and a song combined; some allow you the option to sing two songs, but then you will likely not be considered for any straight plays. The name of this chapter should be, "How much of myself can I squeeze into a 90-second elevator pitch?"

How does one prepare to audition for dozens of theatres, each performing a half-dozen different shows? The short answer is *you can't*. At least, not really.

Sure, you will prepare the same way that you hopefully have for all auditions up to this point. Like every other audition, you should use the best material you have, preferably pieces that you know sell your best attributes and display the biggest range possible. Resist the temptation to go onto the blogs and agonize over the "frequently overdone" lists; don't obsess over what *doesn't work* for other performers. As always, spend your energy focusing on what is the best fit for *you*.

There are, however, a few pieces of homework that will help you maximize your resources. First, you'll want to do a little legwork focusing on the auditions themselves. Some of these are geared towards newcomers to the industry, like StrawHats (which offers only summer, non-union jobs). At the same time, UPTA (United Professional Theatre Auditions) mostly attracts year-round contracts for established professionals. It's not a good use of your time, money, or sanity to stand in a line for hours at a call where the casting directors aren't looking for someone like you.

Also, check the audition websites to see what theatres are attending. Many times, theatres will attend two different conferences, like both NETC and SETC. It doesn't make sense to attend more than one call if the same people see you! Backstage.com publishes a thorough breakdown of dates and requirements every year and offers critical information on:

- Necessary union affiliations and other eligibility requirements (age, education level, etc.)
- Time restrictions and musical parameters
- Professional recommendations required
- Callbacks
- Fees
- Due dates for application (make careful note of these–many combined auditions fill up almost instantly!)

Finally, it makes sense to spend a little research time on what shows are popping up on multiple theatres' seasons. It seems strange, with so many types of musicals out there from which to choose, but certain shows go in and out of fashion at different times. It's possible that half of the theatres for which you audition have all programmed the same Golden Age show or the same new, hip, recently released rock musical. If one of your go-to 16 bars is from a show or in a style you see coming up again and again, it would be prudent to capitalize on the opportunity!

44. Tailoring your union (AEA) audition

Actors' Equity Association (AEA) auditions are not different from non-union auditions, except that if you are a card-carrying member, you can come to expect certain benefits:

- Generally, a lot less wait time and a far more orderly experience with clear sign-up protocols.

- The ability to sign up for a particular block of time for your audition, which makes it far easier to schedule multiple auditions for the same day.

- A better guarantee of at least 60 seconds of performance time, which will allow you to better plan for what selections to bring.

- Believe it or not, only AEA members are allowed to use the restrooms and the nice waiting area in the Actors' Equity building in New York City. If you are waiting at a call for eight or more hours, you will soon see how this is an advantage.

Of course, non-Equity performers can, in theory, be seen at these auditions, but they often have to be in line at the crack of dawn to jockey for a spot in the queue. Also, because they can only be seen when no Equity members are waiting, there is always a chance that they might wait all day and not be able to audition.

The good news is that there are only a certain number of casting directors in New York City. If you start attending AEA auditions, you are eventually going to end up on some important people's radars. Bear in mind, they are not as likely to remember mediocre auditions as they are fabulous ones, so make sure you and your audition songs are truly ready for this step. You'll only have a few chances to make a great first impression with these folks, so you want to make every opportunity count.

45. Tailoring your audition: using recorded tracks

Whenever you are given a choice between using a prerecorded track and a live accompanist, I believe you should almost always use the prerecorded track. I feel it's preferable to know in advance precisely what you're going to hear and know that the accompaniment will be exactly as you've rehearsed it. Years ago, performers would often hire their pianist to meet them at particularly important auditions or callbacks. The in-house pianist who has been sight-reading for several hours appreciated the break, and the singer could enjoy the peace of mind of knowing exactly what the accompanist will be playing. Nowadays, that is rarely done, so a recorded track is the current digital alternative.

If you are in the situation where you can bring a prerecorded accompaniment, make sure that it has been personally tailored to suit your unique rendition. A well-rehearsed backing track sounds like it is following you, not the other way around. The only real way to achieve this is to use a pianist who knows your tempo, your transitions, and the individualized "feel" you have given your song. This is where coaches who are also strong accompanists are particularly useful; they will have the tools both to help you create a strong interpretation as well as the means to tailor the accompaniment to support your choices.

Nowadays, many prerecorded accompaniment tracks can be played right from your smartphone. You also might consider bringing a small set of portable wireless speakers with you, which will make your track loud and clear enough to be heard by you and the auditors. Always double-check that your track works before the day of the audition and consider bringing your music in a variety of formats, like CD or thumb-drive. As a last resort, have a pitch pipe (or a pitch pipe app), so if you have to sing *a cappella*, you'll be able to do so in the key you prepared.

46. Tailoring your audition: agents, managers, etc.

When it's time to pursue professional auditions for employment in the theatre, you'll want to consider obtaining representation to "sell" you to those who can provide employment. These representatives make a commission on the money you earn in the industry, and a trusting relationship is imperative. Actors have the option of either going with an agent, a manager, or both.

Agents are officially licensed to solicit and negotiate employment contracts for their clients. Because they are talent "brokers," agencies filter many, many job opportunities for their clients. More opportunities, however, also means the need for more clients so that agencies can get pretty large.

The upside? A large, well-respected talent agency will usually receive many job notices appropriate for you, but there is the chance you can get lost in the shuffle. Also, because they only make money on commission, most agents aren't going to be interested in you unless it appears that you are ready to work right away.

In recent years, personal managers seem to have become far more common. Managers don't have the power to schedule auditions or negotiate contracts directly. Still, they do provide advice and counsel over your whole career and are more deeply invested in helping you develop as an artist and a professional. They often have much smaller client rosters than agents (a handful as opposed to hundreds), so they can give you much more assistance if something in your career *isn't* working. They'll be more likely to tell you, for example, if you need new pictures, a new acting coach, or, frankly, need to start going to the gym. Many are also very well connected with good singing teachers and coaches and know who you should study with if you're serious about improving your skills and getting more work. Some will even go so far as to coach you for individual auditions and can be especially helpful in assisting in getting you agent representation. They are often the conduit between you and your agent.

Generally, an agent is a necessity in this industry, especially when you get beyond open chorus calls into serious principal auditions and negotiations. Managers, although technically optional, may prove necessary during certain stages of one's career. When performers are first starting out and accumulating experience, managers can be especially worth their cut, and, commonly, managers create the introduction that allows you to ultimately be taken on by an agency.

When auditioning for a specific musical, your goal is to demonstrate your performance compatibility within the style of the show. However, when auditioning for representation, you'll want to show your versatility in whatever musical styles show you off best. As always, you'll want to do well-rehearsed material that suits you and that you know backward and forward. Don't be surprised, though, if this audition seems a bit more casual than other kinds of professional auditions or even a bit *ad hoc* compared to others. It's not unusual that you'll be invited to a space that looks more like an office than a rehearsal space, and you might find yourself singing your heart out in someone's cubicle. Most of the time, if you need accompaniment, you'll need to bring a prerecorded track.

Some managers' client lists are so small, they don't even use a permanent office at all, and might very well interview you down the street at the local Starbucks. Instead of being distracted by the setting, think of these opportunities as a chance for the interviewer to get to know you on a close and personal level. Also, although you ultimately want representation, you should remember that you are interviewing the agent or manager just as much as they are interviewing you. Make sure that you listen very carefully to what they say, heed your gut, and read the fine print before making any commitments!

Helpful advice from legendary agent, Nancy Carson (Carson-Adler Agency):

One of the questions I am most often asked by new people to our industry is, "What is the difference between agents and managers, and are agents the same as casting agents?"

First of all, casting agents, more commonly known as casting directors, are responsible for sorting and presenting talent from various agencies to directors and producers who hire the talent. Of the three, they are closest to the job.

Talent agents represent the actors who they will be presenting to casting. To be a talent representative, an agency must first be a licensed employment agency. The owner must be fingerprinted, background checked, carry a $100,000 bond, and maintain operating and escrow bank accounts. The license must be renewed every three years. An agency also must be franchised by the unions they will work under, Equity and SAG-AFTRA (Screen Actors Guild-American Federation of Television and Radio Artists), to negotiate union contracts. Agents are never paid more than ten percent of an actor's gross salary.

Managers, on the other hand, while also serving a purpose, are not controlled at all. Anyone can hang up a sign and say they are a manager. Managers can help advise clients as well as working hand in hand with the actor's agent to coordinate a busy career. For their service, managers generally charge between ten and fifteen percent. While most actors will need an agent, not every actor needs a manager.

If you think of the job as being the center of a wheel, to get there, you will need to meet the director and producer. To do that, you will need to be seen by a casting director. Your agent will get you to a casting director. A manager can assist you in finding an agent, as well as advise and coordinate what you are doing, but managers cannot, by law, negotiate a contract. Only your agent or an attorney can do that. They are one step further away from the job in most cases, but often can be helpful.

It is important to remember that if you choose to have a manager, you must be careful because there are no controls. Ask many questions and be wary of giving a manager power of attorney over your money until you are sure they are reputable. An agent cannot sign a client for more than eighteen months the first time. Managers generally ask for three years with an option to extend for another two years.

My final advice? Do your homework. It is flattering to have someone want you or your child. Just be sure you also want them.

Nancy Carson is the owner of the Carson-Adler Agency in New York City, well known for representing children and young adults for close to 40 years. As a leader in her field, she began the careers of many of today's stars, including Matt Damon, Ben Affleck, Kristen Bell, Donald Faison, Britney Spears, Ariana

Grande, and so many more. Known as an advocate for young performers, she is on the Advisory Board of the Looking Ahead program at The Actors Fund and has pushed for diversity in casting throughout her career. She is the author of the book "Raising a Star" published by St. Martin's Press.

47. Practice decoding audition listings

When preparing clients for specific auditions, I feel a bit like a detective; part of my job is to help actors find the "secret hidden messages" within the job specifications listed. Due to the subjective aspects of what we do, postings rarely use similar vocabulary. Although casting directors do the best they can to use clear, accurate terms to describe what they're looking for, sometimes their wording can appear confusing or downright contradictory when you're assembling your audition.

Here are a few important areas to consider:

- **Age/Type/Ethnicity**
  - o Age can be relative in this business. Unless the script explicitly states the character's age (where decisions may be "locked-in"), creative teams will have a little wiggle room for the right candidate.
  - o It is against the law for an employer to ask auditioning actors for information about their ethnic background. This will not stop casting directors from making certain presumptions based on your appearance and, in some cases, your name, especially when the script suggests or requires characters to be of a specific race, creed, or

ethnicity. Nowadays, actors worry a great deal about this and whether they appear "_____ enough" to be cast in particular roles. The casting industry is changing rapidly in this regard, and neither my students nor I have any way of knowing what the future will hold.

- **Vocal Range**
  - When specific ranges are listed, such as "needs to belt an E5" (which is the 5th "E" on the piano up from the bottom), do your best to show off your ability in those registers. Don't lose sleep over this, as keys can be changed if the production team is extremely interested in a particular performer, and the word "belt" is highly subjective.
  - Don't be surprised if the actual *Fach* (voice type) listed does not correspond to the range; for example, you might see "Mezzo-soprano who sings to high 'B,'" which would historically be the domain of a soprano. In this case, default to the range listed.
  - No one is interested in hearing you sing notes above your working range. If the show asks for a high G and you only have a great F#, go in and sing the best you can in the key that suits you. Most of the time, finding someone who sounds, looks, and could believably portray the character will be more critical than an exact pitch.

- **Style and Song Selection**
  - Other descriptions, like "soprano belt," "a blend of classical and pop," etc., are, in all honesty, often made up. Because every musical score is a combination of the time and place of the show's writing, along with the time and place depicted in the story, every show has a somewhat unique

style. Try not to get too frustrated over this, because it's challenging to describe sounds in words even if you had pages and pages of adjectives to do it. Casting directors do the best they can with the characters they're limited to in a short job description.

o The word "contemporary" is a relative term and is usually pretty meaningless when it comes to describing audition requirements. Often, it implies that you should do a piece from after the Golden Age of theatre, most likely written in the early 1970s onwards. Remember, though; this has much more to do with the style than what year the piece premiered on Broadway.

Like all jobs, remember that it's up to you to decide what percentage of a job posting you need to meet to apply. Some people are very comfortable going in for job interviews when they have little experience and are happy to roll with the punches during the process. Similarly, some actors will be more comfortable than others going to an audition where the performer is described as a vastly different person than they identify with. As I said before, often casting directors don't always know exactly what they are looking for either, so even if you can only do some of the things required, or only look a bit like the character they've described, consider going in.

48. Grabbing for "brass rings"

Even if you only feel right going to auditions where you feel competitive, I urge you to consider including an "almost there" audition every now and again. This keeps your abilities sharp and allows you to test your marketability with new skills. Have you only taken a few years of tap, but feel that you are one of the top dancers in your class? Try going out for a call that asks for actors who can tap well. Love singing jazz, but only recently started being comfortable singing at open mic nights? Maybe take your strongest piece to an audition and see if it works.

If you start to get callbacks, that tells you that your abilities are strong enough to include as a special skill on your resume and might even lead to job opportunities you had never considered.

Chapter 5

The Accompanist

49. Think of the accompanist as a teammate

Being a great theatre pianist is a bit of a labor of love. Often, if a singer doesn't know his music, he feels justified blaming the accompanist regardless of who was actually at fault. On the other hand, if a performance is brilliant due to the pianist's exacting musicianship, people rarely seem to notice that contribution to the final product. Few performers seem to realize the sheer mental and physical endurance required for these dedicated musicians to do their jobs. Often, they will spend entire days on end sight-reading a dozen different pieces of music an hour in varying states of legibility, handed to them by performers of equally variable ability.

Now, I'm sure any good obstetrician could deliver a baby wherever they happen to be when a patient goes into labor. Still, it's a lot easier in a sterile operating room than in the back of a moving cab. Similarly, these pianists are expected to generate a professional-caliber accompaniment in far from ideal circumstances without even the benefit of a single rehearsal. Many theatre pianists are incredible at what they do, but sight-reading for nervous performers is hardly the easiest situation in which to make beautiful music on the first take.

Therefore, anything you can do to present your music clearly and correctly will decrease the amount of brainpower needed to decipher the needs of the music, thus increasing the level of concentration the accompanist can dedicate to *your* performance. In key number 25, I discussed a handful of tips you can follow to make sure that your music is easy to read and manage. Remember that failing to prepare is preparing to fail–if you want to be the worst audition the pianist has played all day, by all means, bring in single-sided photocopies in the wrong order with notes cut off!

If you have ever worked a customer service job where you dealt with dozens of strangers in the same day, I'm sure you've noticed that there are certain qualities, like respect, politeness, and patience, which tend to result in you going a bit "above and beyond" for that customer. Now, I'm not suggesting any accompanist would ever purposely screw up an audition for a rude or unprepared performer (despite some actors' accusations to the contrary). However, they're only human; thus, the sheer amount of new music they read means that occasionally they will be prone to human error or go on autopilot. I'm not saying that you having impeccable music will guarantee that your music will always be played properly. I am saying, however, that well-prepared music greatly reduces the likelihood of such snafus, freeing the pianist's brain to focus on subtle nuances in phrasing and interpretation. And *those* differences may certainly help a performer to stand out from the pack.

Remember that a mediocre pianist at an audition wasn't just bad for you – every other singer that day will have had the same hurdle to surmount. How you deal with that complication will tell the creative team a lot about what it will be like to like to work with you. If they see you counter a difficult pianist with an obviously good attitude, they are given excellent reason to assume that you will bring the same great energy and professionalism to their rehearsal process. And who doesn't want to work with someone who can skillfully avert problems with a smile?

50. Create functional and straightforward song introductions

The main job of the piano introduction is to inform the singer when to begin singing and on what pitch. If your intro does not accomplish these two things, you need to go back to the drawing board and experiment with different cuts until you feel secure with your entrance each time. Sometimes, the introduction will also set a tempo, and if necessary, give you a way to correct it prior to singing.

Often, a simple "bell tone" (when the piano plays a single pitch that sounds like a struck chime) seems like a good way to begin, and it certainly is an economical use of your available performance time. However, even this very straightforward method needs to be practiced. If a song is in the key of C, starts on an E, and the pianist plays a G bell tone, without sufficient rehearsal, the singer easily might start on the wrong note. Be sure to specify what note you expect to hear.

Many introductions also serve the crucial function of helping the singer transition to the emotional state depicted in the song. You don't need a long time to do this–in fact, I usually recommend a two-bar maximum–but you'd be amazed how hearing a short instrumental phrase can anchor your performance. A rock n' roll vamp, a long-breathed melody, or even a low, rumbling bass note can help establish the feel of the song as well as help you as the actor acquire the dramatic focus to transform into a character before our eyes.

Regardless of what sort of introduction you choose, the most important thing to indicate as clearly as possible in your music is what you want the accompanist to play. Many singers have their music marked at the vocal starting point of a 16-bar cut, but few mark a specific musical introduction. Sometimes they might even say to the accompanist, "Oh, just give me a bar or two." In that case, the singer is following the pianist!

Don't hesitate to highlight instructions, use additional pieces of paper to cover up unnecessary notes, or even use a marker to make your indications painstakingly obvious. Giving your music to a sight-reading accompanist is a good way to see how effective your markings are. Anytime someone is confused by your directions or plays notes that you didn't expect, try to make your music even clearer for the next hardworking pianist.

51. Mark the music exactly how you want it played

All the time you spent learning and rehearsing a song with your teacher, coach, or pianist (live or recorded) may lull you into thinking that the accompaniment will always be exactly what you're used to. When you hear your music played for the first time by a new pianist, it might even sound like a completely different song!

There are things you can do to minimize this problem, even when you haven't rehearsed with the pianist beforehand. For example, the music before the intended vocal entrance can sometimes be misleading; it may be in a different implied key, even though the key signature itself doesn't change. This is especially likely when using music from original rehearsal scores that have not been adapted for solo singers, or if the scene was written interspersed with extended passages of dialogue. In this case, a new introduction may have to be written out for the pianist.

You might notice that there are particular sections of your song where audition pianists seem to be playing the wrong chord. If you notice this happening repeatedly, have a coach who reads music well double-check your score. It's not uncommon that editorial errors work their way into final printed editions. Also, you might notice that there are some songs you love to perform where pianists seem to struggle with the written notes. In these cases, you might try an edition that includes chord symbols above the staff (often included in piano-vocal selections).

Finally, because the introduction to 16-bar cuts must set the tone and the tempo so quickly, you might choose to use a different, truncated introduction than when you are asked to perform a "whole song." I recommend you have two copies of your song, the full version, and the 16-bar shortened audition, cut side-by-side in your book, so you are prepared for both situations.

If an accompanist is unable to decipher markings on music or has multiple unnecessary page turns, your otherwise excellently prepared audition may be sabotaged. The more care you take in the presentation of your audition music, the more care the accompanist will give it. Preparation with a teacher, coach, or accompanist is extremely important, so the singer is not hearing the music on the piano for the first time at the audition.

By the way, have you noticed how many times and in how many ways you've read that particular bit of advice so far? That's because it's extremely important!

52. Minimize the number of page turns in your music

You will want to do whatever you can to minimize page turns for the accompanist. Simply put, playing the piano generally takes *two* hands. This means you want both of the pianist's hands on the actual keyboard as much as possible, not fumbling with pieces of paper. If the audition pianist has to turn multiple pages or manage gymnastic feats like dealing with loose pages on their music stand with music printed on both sides, while attempting to follow directions such as, "Start from the first ending, go back to the verse and cut to the coda," your audition is far more likely to experience insurmountable musical problems.

To remedy this issue, ensure there are no blank pages (i.e., no single-sided copies), and if your selection is longer than two pages, tape, glue, or use sheet protectors to allow your pages to remain back-to-back. If you have repeats or other markings that require the pianist to turn back in the music, I recommend copying the music twice, so all they have to do is turn the upper right-hand corner.

Some accompanists will state their preference for pieces of music taped and laid out accordion-style on hard card stock so that there are no page turns at all. This is easier seen than described, so I recommend that you do a quick web search on "accordion binding" to look at some excellent models with do-it-yourself instructions requiring little more than a ruler and some scotch tape.

A shortcut for beginners would be to simply take your audition cuts from a source like Michael Dansicker's set of *16-Bar Audition Books*, published by the Hal Leonard Corporation. These volumes are generally very well edited, give you a great starting point from which to create solid cuts, and have been specifically edited and typeset to fill two adjoining pages to minimize page turns. Another source of audition cuts is www.musicnotes.com. However, I usually suggest that clients eventually start making their own arrangements rather than always depending on someone else's ideas. There's no guarantee that your best high note or best bit of comedic timing is the same as the performer who test-drove the editor's ideas.

Also, remember, when it comes from a published book, hundreds of thousands of your competitors for a gig will have access to the same piece and arrangement. No matter how brilliant the cut is, there will always be something to be said for originality.

53. Practice giving the tempo and how to cue the accompanist to begin

If you've been to any audition workshops in the past, you might have wondered why master teachers tend to spend so much time dealing with the parts of the audition that occur before any actual singing. No doubt, you've been asked to walk into a room with confidence, "slate" your name and the titles of your pieces clearly, (i.e., "Hello, my name is _____ and I'll be performing _____ from _____") and practice communicating your tempo to the accompanist many times before, all the while wondering, "How difficult can it be to get this right?"

If you sit behind the casting table at an audition, however, you'll see pretty quickly how easy it is for performers to sabotage themselves going through these motions, especially if they don't take the time and care to 1) greet the accompanist calmly and politely, and 2) accurately convey their intended tempo. Nerves are pretty easy to spot when an actor stomps over to the accompanist and bangs out an impossibly fast beat on the top of the piano or snaps their fingers in the poor pianist's face. Neither does a particularly good job of getting the task done.

Instead, you should walk calmly to the piano, and simply give the tempo of your song by singing a bar or two *exactly in the speed and style with which you intend to perform the song* until the pianist confirms they have the information they need. Don't worry about offending anyone by singing these bars out loud; many singers seem to feel like they are supposed to whisper to the accompanist as if it's a secret to anyone in the room that they are about to sing. Remember, you only have a few seconds of practice time–it makes no sense to waste it by misleading (or, worse, irritating) the one person in the room who has the power to make you sound even better.

54. Use songs with straightforward accompaniments

Student Amanda Foto remembers going to an audition and observing that when another girl had forgotten her sheet music, the casting directors asked her to sing "Happy Birthday." She told me, "It's so tough to sound good singing that song that it instilled total fear in me, though I always triple checked that I had my music with me before auditioning. I had brought a piece from Jason Robert Brown's *Songs for A New World* and the accompanist seemed annoyed because that score is very difficult to play. I was scared that I was going to be the next "Happy Birthday" victim, but thankfully he played it anyway – after an obvious eye roll."

In general, it's best to avoid songs with overly complex piano parts that are difficult for the accompanist to sight-read. Many actors deliberately try to seek out underperformed "jewels" of the repertoire to bring to auditions, primarily out of a fear of bringing in an old chestnut that has been deemed overdone. On the one hand, this advice makes sense, and it can be a refreshing change to hear a rarely performed song after dozens of iterations of that season's "flavor of the year." The downside of this approach is that, if a piece is less commonly performed, it is also more likely to be unfamiliar to the pianist, increasing the opportunity for error. If the song is *both* relatively obscure and challenging to play, a rocky audition becomes an even more likely outcome.

Also, when attending regional, local, or school auditions, there is a good chance that the person at the piano is the musical director or even one of the committee members responsible for hiring or admitting you. This individual might be simultaneously attempting to watch you, listen to you, and taking mental notes about how to rank your application throughout your performance. The less amount of thought this pianist must spend on dealing with your sheet music, the more they can spend focusing on your outstanding qualities.

We mentioned earlier that, whenever possible, it can be a tremendous luxury to bring your own pianist. Years ago, it was much more commonplace for singers to hire an accompanist they've rehearsed with to accompany them for their important auditions or callbacks. The waiting area was often filled with almost as many accompanists as performers! This is rarely done nowadays, so you must be extra vigilant about having sheet music that is understandable to a pianist reading it for the first time.

55. Know how to navigate problems

Auditors know you are a human being and that we all sometimes trip up, even in the best of circumstances. It's O.K. Showing the creative team you can successfully rebound from a minor glitch can be a great opportunity to demonstrate your ability to handle inevitable hurdles in a rehearsal or performance with humor and grace. And who doesn't want to hire a performer with that trait?

Part of this skill is about knowing when and if you need to do anything at all. If you make a minor error in your audition, like forgetting to sing a certain embellishment or emitting a minor "voice crack," etc., simply keep going without breaking stride. Usually, the only way a performance mistake will be obvious *is if you make it obvious.* If you don't lose your focus, chances are they will not even notice, much less remember the problem after they've heard your big finish. Remember that they're trying to cast a show, not judge a singing competition.

Mainly, the goal is to address the problem as quickly and painlessly as possible. If the pianist plays a very different tempo than you expect, don't lose your composure. Instead, continue to sing the piece as you prepared it, requiring the accompanist to eventually follow you. If you forget a lyric or invert a few words, don't worry or apologize; just focus on selling the version of the story you told.

Occasionally, you really will find yourself in a spot where a "reboot" is necessary to proceed. In that case, resist the temptation to direct any unnecessary attention to the error by using emphatic apologies, curses, explanations, or mortified glances. Simply stop and politely tell the accompanist what spot in the music to pick up and resume the song as you rehearsed it.

However, if the error was on your part, take a short beat to make sure that the second time through is better than the first. Auditors often see actors stuck in a "mistake loop" who can't work their way out of it after several attempts. Regrettably, this will also tell auditors a lot about a performer's readiness or inability to handle high-pressure situations.

Chapter 6

Bringing Songs to Life
at the Audition

56. Enjoy yourself!

The actor's job is primarily composed of going to auditions, so the best thing you can do is learn to really love them.

This is probably the most commonly overlooked piece of advice in this whole book and may take you some time to absorb and apply. It's no secret that auditions can be tedious in the best of circumstances, and, in the worst, they can be notoriously grueling. When you take away the non-performance elements of an audition, like paperwork, the monitors, and the generally stressful atmosphere, you are left with the very thing that has brought you to this audition in the first place: the opportunity to sing and act for an audience.

Try to remember when you've been waiting in long lines all day that going to this audition has actually given you the opportunity to jump right to your final goal. Sure, it would be nice to be in an expensive costume with a crowd of thousands cheering you on (not to mention a paycheck), but the truth is that you likely came to this profession out of love for singing and music.

Every time you step in the audition room, you have the opportunity to not only do what you love in the long term but also do what you love *today* for a captive, attentive audience. I urge you to revel in every moment.

57. Simply follow the directions

As we mentioned earlier, the language used in casting breakdowns can vary quite a bit. In fact, you might find that different audition listings use completely different methods to describe essentially the same qualities. For example, you might see "high mix belt" on one listing, and "soprano belt" on another, or even "character sings the top line in the score" in a third. None of these three descriptions give you very accurate parameters for the precise range or vocal quality to exhibit during your audition.

You might also see apparent contradictions written into the listing, such as "tenor with fantastic low notes" or "soprano who sings with a classical/pop quality." You might see a job call for a "legit" rock singer, forcing you to decide in context if the use of the term implies that the singer should "sound like a real-life rock singer" or like they should sound in-line with the classical singing tradition. Sometimes you might encounter a call simply looking for "flexible performers," which doesn't give you any real indication of where to start (except implying that whatever you do, try to somehow also do the opposite).

Regardless of the exact description, your best bet is to follow the given guidelines *as literally as possible*. If nothing else, this tactic will provide evidence of your ability to follow directions, which will likely be no small consideration factor to your future employers. If it seems that versatility is being called for, go for as many dramatically different sounds as you can get away with in the context of the same piece. In the case that you are auditioning without specific instructions, such as for a chorus call, you've little to lose by showing off your best, fullest, most reliable high notes. Demonstrating that you can sing more sensationally than is required for the needs of the role, whatever they might be, is rarely detrimental to your audition.

58. Use "common sense"… or do your homework (again)

Your chosen selection must also be appropriate to the show for which you are auditioning. Regardless of how freely the audition listing interprets the term "soprano," one would not choose the same song to audition for Sandy in *Grease*, Laurey in *Oklahoma!*, and Emma in *Jekyll and Hyde*, even if your favorite anthology lists all of these as seemingly interchangeable soprano roles.

As far as what style of piece to bring, a little legwork will allow you to make a more educated guess. I know that you might be getting a little weary of that advice but get used to it—this is a tough industry, and for every hour you spend researching, another actor is probably spending two. I could say just use common sense, but if you don't have the knowledge or experience to make that determination, that's not helpful advice.

So, when in doubt, do everything possible to make an educated decision. Better to sing something written a decade before or after the period of the show's authorship than something written a century later! Sometimes this information is not included in the job listing because the casting director has assumed that the show is in the popular canon and that all performers will be familiar with the score. In this instance, information about the show likely is widely available via a quick web search. Even if there is no cast recording of the show, information about the musical style, the composers, the dates of the original production, and what types of performers were originally cast in the role you're going out for can go a long way to give you a picture of the show's needs.

One last thing: make sure that you've read through the audition directions completely. You might very well fail to notice that at the tail end, the casting director has included some helpful tidbit tucked away like "please, no pop/rock songs." Talk about passing up a time-saver in your preparation!

59. Learn how to move organically

For people who don't particularly care for musicals, their most common argument against the genre seems to be how challenging it is to get past the concept of ordinary men and women, who, going about their daily lives, suddenly break out into heartfelt song. People don't naturally go around singing their thoughts and feelings, these critics protest, and the artificiality of the phenomenon is off-putting.

Unfortunately, I think that a lot of these folks have more than likely been exposed to some pretty bad acting and that it was these bad performances, not the shows themselves or the theatre genre itself, that was responsible for destroying the illusion and promoting such a lifelong distaste for the art form.

True, most people walking down the street tend to not break into emphatic arias at the drop of a hat. However, part of the performer's job is to make this unnatural occurrence seem authentic, natural, and completely feasible within the world of the show. How an actor moves is one of the key components in convincing audiences of their overall believability, and, therefore, relatability.

Have you ever noticed how early attempts at creating realistic, digitized human figures in animated films were never quite "right" looking, despite the millions of dollars spent on making them appear organic and fluid? That is because audiences are highly sensitive to subtleties in movement and expression. Anything that does not appear natural or realistic, like a blink that takes a hundredth of a second too long or a nod of the head that appears slightly faster than ordinary, is rejected immediately as being artificial. Likewise, any theatre actor whose movements appear contrived or empty are unlikely to engage audiences on an emotional level, and therefore never appear truly real.

Genuine body language is *always* truthful. It communicates sincere subtext within songs and reveals your own unaffected physical personality. Spontaneous movement will create a better sense of truthfulness in performance than planned gestures, such as, "I will point downstage left on this line and step forward on this line." That sort of premeditated movement tends to read as synthetic choreography, not a living, breathing performance. Therefore, when singing, you don't need to worry about your hands and arms. Just start with them relaxed and let yourself move exactly as you would in life.

There are two types of movement where "instinctive" tendencies might need a bit of adjustment to augment and not detract from a performance. When the actor is excessively nervous or fidgety, especially when the character she is playing needs to read as grounded and focused, we can often sense the actor interfering with the emerging character. Also, when an actor's body is encumbered by unnecessary muscular tension, movements can appear like those early animated characters that are a fraction of a second off – something the audience will detect right away.

Most schools of acting advise that actors spend some time engaged in movement and body awareness training to make them aware of habitual movements or tensions that ultimately detract from their performance. If you continually receive feedback from coaches and teachers about this, consider seeking out classes in body awareness, allowing you to develop a technique to achieve a more fluid movement quality on the stage.

Many performers also find that some training in improvisation is helpful. After all, when you perform, you're attempting to make rehearsed, prepared words appear extemporaneous. So, the art of coming up with creative and clever improvised scenes may help you develop your natural physical movement in your songs. It's empowering to know you can successfully think on your feet!

Janine Molinari, one of the nation's top choreographers and instructors, advises:

"There is an old saying that applies to actors and singers. Don't move unless, or until you have to! Therefore, my advice is to take a strong stance, hands at your side and forget about them. Begin your performance and trust that your body will move appropriately based on what your character is feeling. Just as in life, we don't plan our gestures and movement when we speak, so it is in performance. Although a simple concept, this can prove to be difficult for many performers.

As a director/choreographer, I often recommend dance and movement classes as a means to teach body awareness and control, which ultimately instills trust in one's physicality. Good posture is an additional benefit of dance class and a necessity in singing properly and acting with strength. The end goal is to move freely and truthfully on stage without having to think about it."

— Janine Molinari

SDC director/choreographer

AEA/SAG-AFTRA

Artistic Director, Broadway's DanceMolinari, NYC/LA/Chicago

Janine Molinari has globetrotted the world as a performer, director, choreographer, master class dance instructor, and guest judge for the televised talent competition Coppa Italia and the upcoming Coppa Europa. She is the artistic director of Broadway's DanceMolinari NYC, LA, CHI, a company that trains young performers for Broadway, TV, films, commercials as well as the music industry.

Her work has been seen in multiple off-Broadway shows, regional, stock, National tours, as well as TV and film. Some credits include Disney's "Kickin It," the Today Show, NBC's COZI TV, off-Broadway's Tony n' Tina's Wedding, Blessings in Disguise, *and the* Totally Tubular Time Machine *starring Debbie Gibson.*

As an Equity, SAG-AFTRA performer, Janine has also sung, danced, and acted in New York, LA, national tours, Canada, Europe, and Asia. Favorite credits include Mary Magdalene in Jesus Christ Superstar, *Tina in* Tony n' Tina's Wedding, *Maria in* West Side Story, *Sarah in* Guys and Dolls, *Smitty in* How to Succeed..., *the west coast premiere of* West Bank, UK *and most recently, Michelle in Off Broadway's* Centennial Casting *in which she won a best supporting actress award. She is the creator of* Tap Out of It, *a new comedy series and the choreographer of* Hooked, *a multiple award- winning series currently in development for a major network.*

60. Know what to focus on, literally and figuratively

I suggest you focus on three specific things during the audition itself: your attitude, your overall goal, and visualizing your imaginary "scene partner."

In a high-pressure situation, it's hard not to be consumed by concerns about the overall outcome. But keep your thoughts in the room itself. Usually, the only result from a first audition is a callback, which should be your primary goal. Be interesting enough that they want to see you again and delightful enough that they already know they'd like to have the opportunity to work with you!

The moment that your audition begins, however, you want to have a clear and specific goal: your dramatic objective. You need to know what you're singing about and to whom you're singing, which will establish your "literal" focus (i.e., how your eyes and face convey your intention). Be able to "see" your scene partner, so clearly, in fact, that you can easily render him or her with only your imagination. If I had to ask you what your scene partner is wearing, where you are together, what time of day it is, what they smell like, and how he or she makes you feel, you should be able to answer without a moment's hesitation.

There are a few schools of thought about where you should physically set your gaze during an audition. Some teachers say never, ever make eye contact with the people behind the table because it makes casting teams uncomfortable. This is especially true if the song is sung to a single imaginary person (e.g., "If I Loved You"). However, if the song is to a pretend group of people (e.g., "June Is Bustin' Out All Over"), it's usually safe to include the people behind the table in that group, glancing at them occasionally like you would members of a crowd.

Like so many areas of this industry, a lot depends on your specific style, as well as the style of the pieces you are performing. If the character you are frequently playing "breaks the fourth wall," you might have more latitude in this area. If you try it out, though, and you find that the folks behind the table look nervous or are avoiding your gaze, try looking at the negative space in-between or over their heads.

61. Check your attitude

When you first walk into the room, appear relaxed and happy to be there. You might be walking into an audition to play a drug addict or a hired assassin. Still, for the moments before the actual audition, you are mainly being assessed as an actor and a human being, not as a character. Try to present yourself as the type of person who they would want to spend an entire workweek with; friendly, professional, relaxed, and, if it's in your nature, fun.

Your attitude when entering the room is the most critical factor in projecting how nervous or confident you appear to others. Your thoughts control your mind, and your mind controls how your body moves. Trying to conceal your nerves forcefully, what some might call taking an "outside-in" approach to performance anxiety, is unlikely to accomplish much except force you to move stiffly and carry a blank facial expression. Instead of giving the appearance that you are at ease, you need to work at being ease.

In all of my decades of working with clients on audition preparation, I've discovered that, for some reason, the most successful performers are those who don't care if they get the part or not. This is not as counterintuitive as it might seem. These singers certainly care in the sense that they will do a lot of preparation on their craft in general, take frequent lessons, practice regularly, and give their all in the audition itself. Still, they tend not to place a lot of undue emphasis on whether or not they book any one specific gig. They trust that the right role will come along if they are patient and hard working.

I realize that this is easier said than done, but the less pressure you place on a single audition, the less your nerves are likely to derail your efforts. You want to make the audition about doing the best work possible and then moving on with your day with a sense of pride in a job well done. Try to embrace the attitude that your real occupation is auditioning, and the opportunity to perform on stage in a show is a potential bonus.

Putting all your eggs in one basket grants the auditioning experience a sort of life-or-death significance that makes it hard to operate with a carefree attitude. Therefore, I urge you to avoid scenarios where this might be the case, like choosing to only audition for one performing arts college without a backup or only auditioning for one casting director. Sure, maybe you'll be incredibly lucky, but even the best performers working today tend to audition many, many, MANY times before being cast.

Placing unnecessary pressure on yourself is a sure way to guarantee you'll be more focused on the outcome of the audition than making the process enjoyable for all involved. If you have a relatively important opportunity coming up, consider auditioning for something else immediately before or after. When these sorts of tasks become a regular part of your daily life, you'll find that they become routine in short order. Then, rather than focusing on rejection, you can enjoy the unexpected opportunities as happy surprises.

62. Enter like a champ

When you prepare to enter the audition room, you need to learn to leave the hustle and bustle of the waiting room, thoughts about the weather, worries around your unpaid electric bill, and any anxieties about how much better your competitors are, behind.

As you go to auditions, try to figure out where the potential distractions tend to crop up again and again and strategize as you go to circumvent the regular pitfalls. For example, if you are the sort of person who other performers naturally enjoy socializing with but would rather enjoy some "alone" time, use earbuds or noise-canceling headphones to listen to music or to buy yourself a few moments of silence. Just stay alert for when the monitor calls your name.

Actors develop all sorts of calming activities, which might include reading, writing in a journal, knitting, texting their friends about lunch plans, etc. Experiment to find what activities are the most effective for you. Similarly, stay mindful of which ones seem to stimulate your nerves in a non-productive way.

For example, I suggest you be careful about how you use your smartphone. Some people might find certain digital applications to be helpful, but I'm sure more than one audition in recent years has been derailed from a poorly timed text message or unfortunate piece of viral news popping up. If you are like most people and find such distractions irresistible, consider taking yourself offline or set your phone in "airplane" mode for the few minutes directly before your performance.

When your name is called, calmly gather your things, take a final breath or two, and enter the room as the best, most powerful, most charismatic version of yourself. From the second you step foot into the room, assume the role of host for your audition. Think of it as YOUR party, and the people sitting at the table are your guests, *not the other way around.* As the host, you're allowed to assume a leadership role, just as you would if you were taking a guest's coat, telling them where to find drinks, or taking the initiative to thank them for a thoughtful housewarming gift. Don't think of it as being overbearing when you walk over to the accompanist to instruct him or her on the tempo. Simply smile and give them the needed information. Don't think you are over-indulgent if you need a moment to establish your focus or need to grab a nearby chair to execute an important piece of blocking. Actors often feel they need to ask permission to perform these tasks, which makes it appear that they don't truly feel comfortable.

Treat the room as if it belongs to you, and you'll convey to your guests that their needs will be met; that it's okay if they sit back, relax, and enjoy your performance. It might be the first time in a very long day of dealing with nervous performers that the auditors get to enjoy a break, and it can go a long way in convincing them that, given the chance, you'll have the necessary skills to put an audience at ease, too.

63. Confidence: real or fake!

Actor/Director Michael Marotta related this experience when directing a production of *Little Shop of Horrors:*

"Trying to find the perfect 'Audrey' for the show, I heard more versions of "Suddenly Seymour" than I care to recount. Most were pretty remarkable, I'll admit, but not exactly what I had in mind. At the end of the day, a girl tripped into the room wearing a skintight black skirt, leopard blouse accentuating a well packaged bra, spiked heels, and hair piled high atop her head. The moment she crossed the threshold, she dropped her book and her music went flying across the floor. Noticeably flustered, she gathered up her scattered things and recovered, sauntered over to the pianist and sang. She wasn't the best singer I heard that day, but it didn't matter; she WAS Audrey! Her timber was right, her entrance a delight and there was no question who our leading lady would be. I offered her the job on the spot."

It's difficult to improve what you can't measure, which is one of the reasons it can be so challenging to develop stage presence. We all know what it's like to watch performers with real stage presence. They seem to radiate an "it" factor that draws your eyes and ears as if pulled by magnets. You might even find yourself describing the experience of watching them sing by exclaiming, "I couldn't take my eyes off of them!" Attractiveness or sheer vocal beauty can certainly play a consideration, but I find it's more about the performer's *overall* appeal.

Despite what you may think when looking at certain television or Hollywood stars, appeal doesn't always mean any specific set of physical or personality traits. Think about how different your five best friends are from each other. Are they all likeable or engaging in exactly the same way? Of course not! Some might be the type that you would love to take with you on a cross-country road trip, and others are better suited to tag along for a night of salsa dancing. Some will be the people you ask for help from if the IRS is auditing you, and others are the types you would ask to have a post-mortem on a recent dating disaster.

Similarly, do the five most beautiful people you know look the same? I highly doubt it. I'm sure if you were to make a list, you would come up with people in all sizes, shapes, colors, etc. There are indeed certain jobs in the theatre industry that might call for very specific physical qualities (i.e., the height requirement to be a Radio City Rockette is between 5' 6" and 5' 10½") to achieve certain on-stage feats. Still, across the theatre world as a whole, I think you'll discover there is a very broad conception of what defines physical attractiveness or marketability.

Different acting roles are going to call for quite different qualities, and you'd be surprised how often the people holding the auditions aren't sure themselves about exactly what they're looking for. They just know that likeability, whether it's the "I'd love to spend a few hours alone with that person," or "I bet I'd really love to hate that person!" tends to win over audiences. In other words, stage presence drives a lot of casting decisions, and confidence is a key factor in emanating stage presence.

Although it can be tempting to try to adapt to what the directors need, you cannot appear confident by trying to be something you're not. A performer's essence will come through regardless of what is said, worn, or sung. If the casting notice is asking for a "quirky, cute, and funny" character and that's not who you are, it is almost impossible to fake those qualities sincerely or compellingly. If the casting directors are looking for a "dark, brooding, mysterious type" and you bound into the room with irrepressibly endearing energy, there's little you can or should do to rectify the problem. This is why at least 50 percent of an auditor's judgement occurs before you've even had the chance to say, "Hello," and probably another 20 percent comes from how you conduct yourself when getting ready to perform. You'll find that, in some ways, these elements reveal more of who you are as a performer than anything you could prepare in advance.

Casting representatives tend to gauge their response to you as an indicator of what future audiences might feel. If they find you funny, enchanting or possessing a certain irresistible "something," they are likely to assume that audiences will feel the same. You're there to sell a product, and the product is YOU. If you don't believe you're good, it will be apparent to everyone watching, so, to quote Oscar Hammerstein II: "Make believe you're brave, and the trick will take you far. You may be as brave as you make believe you are."

64. Be prepared for anything

While I'm quoting, some of my favorite advice is paraphrased from Benjamin Franklin, "Failing to prepare is preparing to fail."

One surefire way to feel more comfortable when auditioning is to make sure you are prepared for almost anything. Things may still come up that are totally out of your control, but as you experience more and more audition situations, you'll grow to be more knowledgeable about what might be asked of you. The key is planning for everything you can so you can walk into the room feeling as prepared as possible.

Learning how to side-step typical difficulties is a skill generally learned over the course of many, many experiences, and, regrettably, these lessons tend to be learned even faster with a small helping of embarrassment. For example, the first time you run out of extra pictures and resumes will probably be the last time you ever go to an audition without spare copies tucked away in your binder. The first time you are asked for a contrasting song, which, as we discussed, is a huge opportunity and advantage for the performer, will probably be the last time you come in without back-up song options. The first time you're asked to stay and dance (when the listing did not mention the possibility of a dance call), and you have to frantically run across town to buy jazz shoes, will definitely be the last time you don't toss an extra outfit in your bag when headed out to an audition. But it's okay to make mistakes, as long as you learn very quickly from them. You'll find those same people to be a lot less understanding if you come in as unprepared the second, third, or twentieth time.

"I was in the middle of a show, offstage, when I got an email from my agent for an audition in under 48 hours. It included about 50 pages of sheet music for a show that I was somewhat familiar with, but didn't know musically at all. I initially responded to my agent saying that, with two shows the next day, I didn't have the time to learn all of the material to go in and sing it competitively. To his credit, my agent responded saying that I had to go in and do whatever I needed to do to learn the material. So, I did. I booked last minute sessions with my audition coach and my singing teacher, and I spent all the time I wasn't working on preparing the material. I sang it at home until it was too late to be belting it out, and I listened to the music on my commutes to and from work. I barely slept or ate because it was such challenging music and I needed every single minute of preparation to be able to perform it at top level. I got the job, which became my second Broadway credit!"

– *Celia Mei Rubin, Broadway Performer*

65. Plan, but don't place undue importance on the cosmetic stuff

Although we live in a society that claims to value the beauty within, there is a whole lot of judging books by their cover in the entertainment industry.

I certainly had to think about this tendency (both literally and figuratively) when publishing this book. What sort of message was I looking to put out there for prospective readers? How could I grab the attention of serious performers without looking like I was pandering to make a sale? Things like the layout on the page, the format, even the title would give students not already part of my studio a sense of my teaching philosophy, and I needed to be very careful to choose words and images authentic to me.

However, let's be fair: there are lots of amazing books out there with dreadful covers, and every year, hundreds of fabulous novels end up in the clearance bin due to poor marketing choices. Sometimes they make it to the bestseller list despite an off-putting design, but usually, covers that remain on message end up with the best critical and commercial reception. That means that time and expert care is taken to make sure the content and packaging reflect each other's essence. Some of the worst covers I've seen are those that try too hard to sell the goods inside with splashy quotes or dramatic images. Some of the best I've seen are simple, where every element, down to the font, reflects the tone of the whole.

Similarly, a performer should think about whether their outsides reflect their insides. Your personal style is important and likely reflects the sum of the unique qualities that casting directors will specifically want to cast you for. Just make sure to 1) establish a "clean and neat" version of yourself, and 2) if possible, wear clothes that don't *prevent* you from appearing as a character in the show.

This isn't as complicated as it sounds. Just like any interview, you'd do well to show that you've mastered basic grooming, especially in situations where you are working near other people. If you have had trouble with this somewhat necessary life skill, consult a trusted friend. This is information you want to have. However, different characters call for different looks. If having your hair up or down, shaving or going unshaven, wearing glasses or contact lenses, etc. allows you to feel more like a specific role, then go for it, as long as the overall look wouldn't be noticed as unusual when you walk down the street.

You'll also want to think about clothing choices that don't say "costume," but allow the producers to project their imagination onto you like a canvas. There's no need to roll around in dirt before auditioning to be a beggar in *Les Misérables*. Still, perhaps for this audition, you might choose something casual, modest, and somewhat representative of the time period. Ditto for your footwear; closed-toed shoes pretty much look like closed-toed shoes from any era, but if you wear Nike sneakers to play a character two centuries before those shoes were invented, you might pull an interested director out of the scene. Maybe, in this scenario, women should consider forgoing their typical immaculate, pin-straight blowout, and let their hair take on its natural (and more period-looking) wave. Men might forgo shaving for a couple of days or being a little less liberal with styling gel, nothing so dramatic as to make others in the waiting room afraid to sit next to you, but enough to affect the "buyer" on an unconscious level.

66. Take the time to reflect afterwards

There is no doubt that auditions can be stressful, and it's perfectly natural to walk out of the room and wish to shake off the whole experience and move on with your day. To some extent, this is a healthy impulse; it's important to let go of events over which you no longer have control.

However, I encourage you to develop strategies directly following every performance or audition to briefly reflect on how you did. If you don't, you inadvertently deny yourself a great learning opportunity to identify both what went well–in other words, celebrate a job well done–as well as identify what elements you might want to tweak for the next time.

If you prepared for an audition with an instructor, it's often a nice gesture to contact that person and offer your assessment of what happened on the big day. Personally, after helping a singer prepare for an audition, I want to find out how it went. I'm not just being polite or making small talk when I say, "Let me know how it goes!" I find it helpful to unpack the events of auditions to help establish goals to work on while the lessons of the last ordeal are still fresh in your mind.

At the very least, I'd consider journaling after the experience, listing details about what you sang, how you felt, and any variables you can think of that you'd want to repeat next time, as well as those that you will try to avoid in the future. This includes what you wore, any distinctive hair choices, and anything unusually helpful or harmful to how well you felt. If your audition results in a callback, you'll want to look like the same person they liked at the initial audition. Did you finally find a set of audition shoes that made you feel poised and comfortable, or did you find that eating that high-protein lunch helped you focus? Maybe you had to skip lunch out of necessity and found, for the first time, that your tummy was butterfly-free in the audition room. Perhaps you had an extra shot of espresso in your latte that made your heart pound in your chest before the audition, and now you know you need to opt for decaf next time, or maybe you found a clearer copy of that rarely done song you've been working on, and, for the first time, the accompanist played the piece flawlessly. All of these are worth writing down and remembering.

Like most new activities, you might find that you need to formally ritualize such reflection for it to become habit. However, you need to determine what works best for you. Try to keep the narrowest window possible in between the event and the reflection, so you have the best chance of recalling salient details.

Unfortunately, high adrenaline, the sort that accompanies both great (and not-so-great) auditions, tends to cause many performers to have the critical memory of a goldfish. Chances are that you will soon forget much about what happened at the audition or performance. That's a shame, considering how hard you prepared. Making sure you reflect accurately and log your reflections will maximize your learning curve and ultimately leave you more empowered over the process.

67. Do listen to others' feedback, but consider the source

Competitive singing shows and other types of variety programming have done some great things for the entertainment industry, allowing many talented newcomers to rise to stardom overnight. However, I find one downside of this trend is the "everybody knows best" phenomenon where, after binge-watching a few seasons, many of my clients consider themselves something of a savant. "I can do what these judges do! I don't need to pay some expert for their advice," they might think.

You have to understand that, on these shows, taping sessions on "elimination day" can last all day long. Countless hours of thoughtful adjudication by knowledgeable, experienced specialists are often edited down to a few minutes, highlighting the most scathing, flattering, or clever tidbits for the amusement of the home audience. These folks frequently really know what they're doing, but the sort of discipline-specific verbiage that requires a decade of schooling to understand tends to make for rather dry network television. On the actual sound stage, performers most likely received hours of careful, considered analysis of their singing, but all the home viewers got to see was the wrinkled nose of a celebrity curmudgeon calling the performer "pitchy."

Incidentally, "pitchy" is not a musical term; it's an example of non-threatening language concocted by producers so that the audiences at home (non-musicians included) can feel involved, and perhaps even think, "Wow... being a judge looks sort of easy!" I assure you, it's not. It took every bit of the last three decades to learn what I know about singing and performing, and even now, I continue to learn something new most every day.

Unfortunately, in our "reality show world," I find that students (and their parents) sometimes show up to lessons with highly preconceived notions about what kinds of songs they should sing and how they should sing them. Whether or not they realize it, a lot of these notions have been formed by the sorts of performances that play well in thirty-second excerpts on TV but fall flat when it comes to professional auditions.

Nowadays, because of the singing performances that stand out in these highly edited TV situations, some clients want only cutting-edge, show-stopping repertoire or songs with super high belting and tons of riffing. In these cases, I tell my students that while I appreciate their enthusiasm, they may be laboring under a few misconceptions about what constitutes a good performance with healthy and aesthetically pleasing vocal production. Also, sometimes what a casting director might be looking for is someone with a voice that will blend well with the rest of the ensemble.

It is true that singing performances are not just about what the performer feels but what they make an *audience* feel. Acquiring varied, insightful feedback from both professionals and non-professionals (i.e., the lion's share of any Broadway audience) is a great way to assess how impactful your performance strategies are. However, I urge clients to always contextualize such remarks based on the background, motivations, and intentions of the opinionated parties, as well as your specific relationship to those individuals. Are they a teacher, or do they have an extensive background with musicians and singers? Are they using helpful language that empowers you by shedding light on specific components of your performance, or do they resort to only "good" or "bad" evaluative statements?

On the other hand, be wary of the kind of feedback that is more likely to frustrate than help you. If the remarks originate from family members, do they tend to get under your skin regardless of the situation? Is the feedback coming from an acquaintance or colleague with whom you might be a bit more of a "frenemy" than friend? Could it be someone who consciously or unconsciously would have any sort of incentive to see you flounder a bit? If so, tread very, very carefully.

68. Avoid overthinking

This is another important one in the "easier said than done" category. However, the ability to change gears from reverse to drive after an audition or important gig is essential to have a lasting career in this business.

After you finish your audition, just move on. Beyond the aforementioned short recap with your coach, resist the temptation to overanalyze the audition outcome. Obsessively replaying mental footage will only result in frayed nerves, increased anxiety, and accelerated burnout, as well as drive everyone close to you crazy. Leave counterproductive, neurotic thoughts to stage moms, insecure divas, and all the other folks who are not long for this industry.

For example, let me tell you a story about one of my long-time clients who has performed on Broadway and in leading roles throughout the country. While still a teenager and new to show business, she was up for a leading soprano role in a major theatre. It required her to sing in a "legit" head voice, which was how she had been trained. While waiting to hear about that job, she was offered a "belt" role on a major cruise line, which she didn't want to accept. She started to practice belting in an exceedingly, loud, high manner that she assumed was required. Unfortunately, without much experience in how to make the registration shift safely, she injured her vocal folds. Her otolaryngologist gave her some steroids to reduce the swelling of her vocal folds. Ironically, this medication made her fail the cruise line drug test, and during that time, she was offered the leading soprano role she originally desired!

These sorts of rapid twists and turns are not unusual in this industry, and there is little an actor can do to be prepared for every eventuality. Fortunately for my client, she was wise enough to realize her mistake in attempting to force her voice to do something it wasn't ready for, listened to her doctor, and was ready to work when she received the surprise phone call.

The sooner you can learn to quickly and efficiently assess your performance and press on towards the next great opportunity, the more balanced, sustainable, and enjoyable your career, and life as a whole, is likely to be.

Chapter 7

Audition FAQ

69. Which songs would you tell a client to avoid?

It is very typical for young performers to fret about whether their preferred song is overdone. More experienced singers tend not to worry so much about this because their years in the trenches tell them that well-known pieces are often fantastic showcases for their abilities. Just like some unknown songs and shows have been forgotten for a reason, sometimes well-known pieces are frequently performed because they just *work!*

Remember, they don't hire the song, they hire the singer. At a successful audition (i.e., an audition in which a performer earns a callback), it's not uncommon that the actual song that earned the callback will be instantly forgotten because the casting directors have mentally moved on to the role the actor might win in their specific show.

However, there is one category of songs that you might want to consider performing only in rare circumstances: the signature song. Sometimes a performance is so iconic, so masterful, that it is difficult for the next couple of generations of listeners to separate the performance from the performer. Barbra Streisand in *Funny Girl* certainly fell into this category, as did Kristen Chenoweth in *Wicked* or Ben Platt in *Dear Evan Hansen*. Sometimes iconic performances can even unseat other iconic performances in the public eye, like when my former client, Lea Michele, sang "Don't Rain on My Parade" on *Glee*. Still, in the years following the airing of that very popular episode, I would advise any client who didn't sing the song as well as Lea (or Barbra) to consider if there is a better option in their book that might become their own "signature." Generally, I would recommend staying away from any song currently running on Broadway. No need to have your audition performance compared with the original cast recording, which has had the benefit of careful sound mixing (including a bit of auto-tuning here and there), a full orchestra, and multiple takes.

Use the same tools that you might use for any other song to evaluate if someone else's signature song works for you. If the song feels right to perform in virtually every situation, helps you sound amazing, highlights your uniquely winning qualities, and almost always wins you a callback, it's probably a keeper.

70. Does that mean we should find obscure songs that no one else sings?

Often, clients ask if I know audition songs that no one else sings. I tell them that's not always the best choice. Casting directors have spent entire days, decades, or even whole careers listening to different renditions of "Tomorrow" and "On My Own" and still manage to spot the best performances out of hundreds of mediocre renditions. In fact, I think having a casting director think, "Boy, that was the best interpretation of that song I've heard in years," is a pretty desirable response in any audition situation.

It's not a bad idea to use classic songs that are so good that the listener remarks, "Gosh, I wish more people sang that piece!" The fact that you had to dig a little through the repertoire to find such a gem also suggests that you know your stuff and take your craft very seriously. You might allow the panelists to enjoy a bit of nostalgic reverie in the course of a long, hard day of auditioning, and it's even possible that they might take special notice of the singer who has demonstrated the unusual taste to look beyond the top hits of that season.

If you are singing an unfamiliar piece, it's probably a good idea to tell them what you'll be singing and where it's from. After all, you want the auditors listening to YOU, not spending your two minutes of performing time distracted, and trying to place what show the song is from.

Also, you'll want to account for the chance that accompanists may have more trouble playing a song they have never seen or heard before. To compensate for this, once again, make sure your music is impeccably clear and follows some of the formatting guidelines mentioned in earlier chapters. If possible, adding chord symbols might help with sight-reading. In case the sheet music is only available in a semi-legible handwritten manuscript, you might have to work with a copyist to create a clear arrangement.

71. "I'm so scared of auditions – Help!"

I have seen many students who show great potential but are crippled by feelings of self-doubt. I call them the "I-Think-I-Can't" students. They have internalized the belief that they're just not the sort that can step outside of their comfort zones no matter how many times they are assured by their teachers that they exhibit strong potential.

Singing in public requires, to a certain degree, being uninhibited with a willingness to wade into the unknown and explore the boundaries of one's own voice and personality. It's no surprise that students who doubt themselves often find the technical and emotional requirements of singing to be difficult or even impossible. Stopping this game of mental sabotage is crucial to achieving your goals and a valuable life skill.

There is no one-size-fits-all solution to instilling confidence in a student. It may take a few weeks (or longer) just to begin to scratch the surface of what is getting in the way. Some students tell me they don't believe they're able to sing; however, I tend to believe that when people take the trouble to make an appointment with me and pay hard-earned money for a lesson, they must have at least a trace of a belief that improved singing is possible for them.

Examine your past, your mental habits, and how you have overcome various obstacles in your own life. Are you the sort who needs a bit of a push into the deep end of the pool? Are you the kind of student who moves slowly but can make substantial changes over months or years with a knowledgeable guide? This is one of the many reasons why your choice of a teacher can be so important towards your evolution as a singer and a person.

72. The waiting room

I don't think anyone looks forward to hours spent in audition waiting areas (otherwise known as "holding pens"). Any anxieties you're feeling often multiply while surrounded by so many others who are after the same role you are. Some in the room want just to mind their own business and focus on their upcoming audition. Others let their nervous energy out by striking up unwelcome, mindless conversations with everyone around them, or, worse, deliberately undercut others with passive-aggressive remarks.

Think of the waiting room as a professional workspace, and don't let others distract you from your impending audition with negative gossip or self-important behavior. Remember that their behavior–not yours– is what should be considered out of place in this environment. Ignore their assertions that they know the "real scoop" on what the auditors are looking for, such as, "Well, they're only looking for girls over 5' 10" tall, or, "They really can't use you if you can't belt over a G." You know from earlier keys that things constantly change in the audition room and that any effort to reveal the "real" gossip will likely only derail your efforts and instincts. Try not to engage in such rubbish and worry about the only thing you have direct control over: your OWN audition.

By the way, when you're standing outside the audition room, everybody else seems to sound great through the closed door. Don't let it freak you out. Instead, assume that everyone else is huddled around the door when you sing, intimidated by how good *you* sound!

73. Even when the initial audition goes well, callbacks scare me to death!

It's certainly understandable that callbacks could be intimidating. You're one step closer to booking the gig, which may have some people feeling the weight of increased pressure.

However, when you think about it, that's a "glass half empty" attitude. I encourage you to look at a callback from a positive perspective, and remember that you've already proven yourself adequately skilled for the job, or they wouldn't have called you back! At this stage, they are comparing different possibilities for a role, but you can only do the best you can at what you do. I often say that, at this point, a lot of your success will be based on look and luck. Just deal with factors that are in your control, like knowing your music, getting adequate rest in the days leading up to the callback, staying hydrated, and committing to the best acting performance possible.

One additional piece of advice: if they sent you material to prepare, learn it as flawlessly as possible. However, don't feel the need to memorize every word unless specifically instructed to. If you happen to memorize them while working on them, that's all the better, but keep the script or score in your hand for insurance. It would be unfortunate if a great performance were derailed by something as minor as a memory slip. Also, it serves as a visual reminder to the auditors that this was recently learned, that your performance isn't in any way "set," and that you are open to receiving direction.

74. What should I bring with me to auditions?

For starters, bring your book of audition music. Since your book is never really "finished," most singers use 3-ring binders that can easily be rearranged. For your entire career, you'll probably be changing your mind about exactly which songs to include in your audition repertoire. You'll also probably be adding material that suits specific audition requirements, and removing what no longer works for you, or songs you've simply grown tired of singing. It's a good feeling to know that you're ready for practically every audition situation. You'll always have contrasting back-up songs at the ready, and will never need to worry about what types of songs to bring with you again.

A couple of other things to have on hand in your audition bag: always, always, always have a few extra photos/resumes with you as well as a pair of dance shoes and a quick change of clothes tucked away. You'd be amazed how often you're asked to do a movement combination when it wasn't mentioned in the audition listing.

Also, as you go to auditions more frequently, you'll likely start storing a mini supply cache of little emergency items that might make a big difference to your confidence in a pinch. Things like a water bottle, some snacks, a toothbrush, needle and thread, extra contact lenses, aspirin, Band-Aids, and focusing tools like a stress ball or deck of cards can be lifesavers. Six-hour wait times are long enough, and without certain critical items, they will seem even longer.

75. How can social media HELP my career?

When I began working with singers, little of the technology we now take for granted existed. We only had to worry about "word of mouth" and what was published in newspapers and magazines. I eagerly embrace technological advances, and I was one of the first voice teachers to create a professional website. It didn't take long before the paper newsletters I used to send out became digital, and I was an early participant in any online social media that would help me connect with my students and colleagues. It's made a really big difference in allowing students from all over the country to find me when they make trips to New York City. And with the ability to do lessons online, I have the opportunity to teach students from all over the world.

Similarly, innovative programs and apps have made it easier and more inexpensive than ever for performers to seek out job listings, which the performing arts community will often help disseminate via actors' own social media feeds. Many times, you can submit your headshot and resume as attachments (saving lots of postage and printing costs in the process). In some cases, you can audition for a job digitally using only online videos (known as "self-tapes").

76. How can social media HURT my career?

Bear in mind, though, this kind of accessibility can be a double-edged sword. Cyber alternatives may have allowed performers to have less expensive and easier access to opportunities. Still, it also allows their prospective employers to have similarly direct access to actors' private lives. We'd like to think that we are permitted separate "personal" and "professional" identities on principle. Still, the truth is that theatre people work very, very closely together, and that line can get blurry. Actors should assume that they will have your name searched, and more will be known beyond how well you act, sing, or dance. If red flags come up on your public profiles, they will be seen and considered.

It is also critical to be wary of what you say on the internet, even in places where you would never think that professionals would look. Let me give you one example from the early days of online chatrooms in the 1990s. I had just seen a new Broadway musical that I didn't care very much for, with music written by a very well-known and established composer. I was very candid, and typed a scathing review, detailing everything I disliked about the music, the lyrics, the story, the set, etc. for the whole world to see. I found out through the grapevine that the composer, who I had never met in person, had seen my post and was furious at me! I never dreamed that he would see the post, remember my name, or care what I thought of the show. Not the way to make a positive first impression, I learned in no uncertain terms.

The lesson is this: be very discerning about what you put online. Will someone who's thinking of taking you on tour want to know that you're a party animal who drinks every night of the week, or that you're fond of making off-color jokes about castmates or trash-talking former directors? Absolutely they will, and this information will, without question, be used against you. Similarly, if you are a good, decent, well-rounded person who takes pride in their work, contributes to their community, and is supportive of fellow artists, that will become apparent in the digital trail you leave behind you.

Also, it might surprise you to hear that there is a new generation of stage parents who write social media posts under their kids' names, or performers whose pages are written by their managers. It's pretty obvious when this is the case and does little to further anyone's goals. In general, I'd advise performers to wait until they really, truly have content to share with the world before feeling the need to establish a digital persona. And, when you are ready, remember the aphorism: "Unless you have something nice to say, refrain from saying anything at all."

77. Should I sing a song from the show?

I recommend singing a song from the show you're auditioning for *only if it is specifically requested*. That way, you don't inadvertently limit yourself to being considered for only that particular role. Also, you don't want to appear locked into a specific performance, which might not match the director's vision for a given character. This has been known to happen even if a director doesn't yet consciously know what they're looking for!

When preparing to audition for a specific show, look at the part or parts you're most likely to be cast as based on age, physical type, and vocal range, then skim through your book to find a current song in your repertoire that most closely resembles those vocal demands. For example, if you were going in for a *My Fair Lady* call and were a good type to play the role of Eliza, another Lerner and Loewe ballad, such as one of Guinevere's songs from *Camelot* or another similar Golden

Age song, would help demonstrate to the casting directors what they need to know about your ability to sing the role.

You also might explore an individual performer's discography to determine good audition song possibilities. For the above example, you might take a look at recordings made by others who have played the role of Eliza, including Julie Andrews, Christine Andreas, and Melissa Errico, to give you an idea of what repertoire selections might show the casting directors your vocal strengths.

There's no harm, though, in having songs from the show on-hand in your book, too! If you happen to kill it on "The Simple Joys of Maidenhood," it's not unheard of that the director may ask you to sing a few bars of "I Could Have Danced All Night" or "Wouldn't It Be Loverly" to help them decide if you need to be called back.

78. What if the person right in front of me sings the same song?

Avoid changing songs at the last minute, period. Chances are that the instinct to throw your plan out the window is just your mind's attempt to quell your nerves and regain control over a potentially uncontrollable situation. Don't fall for it.

It's natural to second-guess yourself when under pressure, and at first, it's a bit scary to trust yourself. Remember what I said about your song choice not making or breaking an audition. How well you sing, though, is still of critical importance. It seems unlikely that you can do your best work without having fully prepared.

Trust your preparation and training, and what you do *well*. Consider what might happen if you deliver the best rendition of a particular song the folks behind the table haven't heard in years. Then become that singer who nailed "such and such" in their memories, which is an enviable place to be when a callback is on the line.

79. What if I'm specifically asked to sing *a cappella*?

I advise you to avoid singing *a cappella* whenever possible. If given a choice between bringing a pre-recorded track and singing solo, always, *always* use a track. Just make sure to have practiced with it extensively before the big day, so you are familiar with it. To make the track perfectly fit your performance, try to have someone custom record an accompaniment that suits your interpretation of the piece. If you use a commercial karaoke track, it can be edited to suit your specific performance, including cuts and key changes.

Of course, there may be times where the decision is out of your hands, and solo voice is strictly requested. This is not uncommon in certain situations, such as large open calls for reality television shows, for agent or manager auditions in a small office, or in school music programs where the only available pianist in the room–the music teacher–might also be directing the show. Be aware that if you begin the song in the wrong key, you could run into some sort of insurmountable vocal trouble down the line. It can be helpful to listen to the melody right before you sing to refresh your ear, so carry a recording with you.

Also, it might be useful to know the first pitch of the song, which will be a letter from A to G, possibly followed by "flat" or "sharp." Sometimes there is a piano in the room that can be used to refresh your starting note. You can also play it yourself via blowing into a pitch pipe–the old-fashioned way–or via an electronic pitch pipe app available on your phone. And, it's never a bad idea to be able to find the note on the piano yourself.

80. What if I can't decide on 16 bars, or my song is awesome when uncut?

Not every piece pares down well. Sometimes you'll try out dozens of different versions, cutting and pasting together all sorts of different arrangements, but will never quite come up with a sixty-second arrangement that sounds like it has a true beginning, climax, and a satisfying conclusion. This is often the case with "story songs," which are constructed with a longer narrative arc in mind that can't be conveyed in any single one-minute excerpt. These types of pieces, like "Stars and the Moon" from *Songs for a New World* or "Meadowlark" from *The Baker's Wife,* make for wonderful cabaret and recital selections, but rarely make for good 16-bar auditions. To draw an analogy to television, think of story songs as long-form miniseries, as opposed to stand-alone scripted comedies or dramas better equipped to communicate a complete story in less than thirty minutes.

Some performers will simply bring a complete song to auditions anyway, determined that their unparalleled artistic genius will win over the panel and buy them more time. I recommend that you not assume this will happen. Trying to get through your entire song when only asked for 16 bars mostly shows that you don't know how to follow directions, and warns the creative team that you might be equally obstinate during the rehearsal process if offered the job.

However, if you do really well on a cut that leaves them hungry for more, it is entirely possible you may be asked for a second selection, maybe even a full song. In this instance, it would be very smart to have that epic story song copied, in your book, and ready to go!

Chapter 8
Managing Your Career

81. Understand the role of family in career management

Regardless of your age, work/family/life balance needs to be considered when pursuing a career in the entertainment industry. The uncertainty of steady employment, the inevitable expenses, and the unavoidable emotional tolls are all realities that you will have to face.

Perhaps the first image that comes to mind when thinking of the family's role in building a career is Rose, the quintessential stage mother, barging on stage screaming, "Sing out, Louise!" at her shy, quiet daughter during the opening scene of *Gypsy*. Stage parents often get a bit of a bad reputation. They are frequently characterized as pushy, annoying, meddling, gossiping individuals who will stop at nothing to help their children get ahead in show business. Well, yes, I've encountered a few of those types of parents, but in my experience, they have been in the minority. During my years in the industry, most of the parents I've come into contact with have behaved professionally, fairly, and were dedicated to doing anything necessary and appropriate to help their children achieve their career goals.

On the other hand, despite providing piano accompaniment for thousands of auditions and having clients in virtually every musical running on Broadway today, you wouldn't believe how many parents think they know better than I do about what their child should be singing! Personally, I welcome parental input, but only if it is constructive and supportive, especially in front of their kids.

Many parents ask me if their child has the "potential" to pursue a career in show business. I feel that my job isn't really to judge, but to help all my students perform as well as they can. Like we said earlier, whether it leads to a paying job depends on many things that are out of a performer's control, the biggest two being *luck* and *look*.

Young performers must rely on responsible adults for so many aspects of this business: to schedule and subsidize lessons, travel with them to auditions, rehearsals, and performances, and, most importantly, to keep them safe and healthy. But another essential component of being responsible parents in the entertainment industry is to provide a safe haven for their children's inevitable fears, uncertainties, hurts, and disappointments that are part of this business. My friend and colleague Denise Simon's book, *Parenting in the Spotlight: How to Raise a Child Star Without Screwing Them Up* has a lot to say about this. If there are budding professionals in your charge, I strongly urge you to read it.

Another helpful reference is *Raising a Star: The Parent's Guide to Helping Kids Break into Theater, Film, Television, or Music* by experienced talent agent Nancy Carson. In this book, there are answers to many of the day-to-day problems that come up for young performers. Topics include auditions, resumes, how to avoid the devastating frustrations that come with a career in show business, and, most importantly, how to allow kids to look natural at auditions and interviews.

Confessions of a Casting Director is the definitive guide to breaking into film, television, theatre, and even YouTube from longtime casting director and studio executive Jen Rudin. Packed with information that aspiring actors need, her up-to-the-minute expert advice is essential for anyone pursuing an acting career. Jen Rudin demystifies the often intimidating and constantly changing audition process, sharing insider tips on preparing for every type of audition: theatre, television (including commercials and reality TV), and film to voiceovers, animated movies, and even web series.

In my experience, most show business kids will not end up pursuing performing careers as adults. Whether they end up in related fields such as casting, producing, management, directing, or writing, or some entirely different career path, the valuable confidence they develop being able to get in front of people will serve them well.

82. Treat your business like a business

Professional relationships are not that dissimilar from personal relationships. I have worked with some of my clients for decades, and am proud that at this stage in my teaching career, I am occasionally coaching the children of former child clients.

Therefore, when it comes to your support staff, I have to confess to being a bit of a loyalist. If a student or client is struggling, it is so easy to blame the instructor. Yes, people shouldn't be afraid of making a change when necessary, but I'd rather approach it from a "how can we make this work" angle. You'd be surprised how many times a simple communication block is to blame for a plateau, or how often a short sabbatical from lessons might allow a student to return refreshed and refocused.

However, if, over a long period of time, a certain professional relationship is no longer moving you forward, it is really important to know how to do some deep reflection and identify when something just isn't working out. As you grow and change throughout your career, I would hope that your ability to assess your own wants and needs would also improve. As a client, you need to invest your resources where they will do you the most good.

This is also important advice when it comes to your management team. Perhaps you feel a sense of duty towards your first agent or manager for having discovered you, but now that you are becoming more established, you know that you are not getting competitive auditions suitable to your ability. It may feel a bit like you are "biting the hand that fed you," but think of it this way: chances are, that representative is also really, really good at helping new professionals start their careers and perhaps not so good at helping mid-career performers. By being honest and moving on when the time is right, you are opening their schedule for a client they are better equipped to help while allowing yourself to find an office better suited to your needs.

Chapter 9

Your Continuing Education and Achieving Your Goals

83. Do create and revisit your goals regularly

It's very hard to predict where your career will lead. Almost all of my most successful clients originally came to me because they were planning to begin their careers on Broadway, but I think we can safely assume that when I list names like Ariana Grande, Natalie Portman, Sarah Jessica Parker, and Britney Spears, the reader is unlikely to think of them as young, unknown musical theatre actors working on landing their first major roles. You cannot compare their career paths, as each was unique with different twists and turns, and each had entirely different experiences in the recording studio, on television, and in Hollywood. Similarly, I do not believe it is wise for performers to set out attempting to re-create someone else's career, or to use any celebrity's successes as a yardstick to measure their accomplishments.

Achieving "success" really depends on how you define it. It's important that you try to create quantifiable, actionable goals at every step of your journey. You can't improve what you can't measure. It's a good idea to do this periodically, maybe every six months, and take stock of which goals you are getting closer to. This way, you can create "action items" that allow you to more quickly and easily attain those goals.

Here are some examples from which a newer performer might benefit:

- Establishing a regular practice regimen (e.g., I will practice a certain number of times a week, a certain number of minutes).

- Dedicating a certain number of hours to taking in masterful performances, such as attending more professional productions and watching film versions of classic musicals.

- Increasing the number of auditions you attend and trying out some of the earlier strategies in this book to help you land more callbacks.

- Finding more opportunities to sing in front of people. It could be at a piano bar, karaoke, talent competition, or religious service, as long as you get up in front of people, so that it becomes as close to second-nature as possible.

Don't be afraid of "low-hanging" fruit; when a performer is first starting, it's advisable to set goals that are largely within your control, like the number of lessons a month you want to attend or the number of practice hours a week you plan to commit. Try not to place your goals in the hands of factors that may be outside your control, such as "I'm going to win a Tony Award for Best Actress in the next five years" (although you *should* feel free to prepare yourself for stardom by sharpening your skillset as much as possible).

Maybe in the next month, you want to perform your first belt piece, in which case your teacher may be able to guide you towards options that will be suited for your current abilities while challenging you, or maybe you want to begin stretching your range higher or lower, in which case your coach will know your voice and how far is healthy to stretch. You'll find that speaking with an expert might help you identify aspirations that you didn't even know you possessed.

84. Remember, there is always the next audition

When you read biographies of your favorite famous performers, it's easy to get the impression that all of them received some sort of "big break" due to being in the right place at the right time. True, there is an element of luck that is involved, whether you define luck as something celestial or a statistical anomaly. But I've also discovered that someone who goes to 200 auditions seems to somehow have a better of chance of "being lucky" than someone who goes to two auditions, gets frustrated, and calls it a day.

Even if you don't believe in luck, it's pretty easy for a mathematician to prove why the likelihood of getting what you want increases in exact proportion to the number of chances you take and the number of positive decisions you make. Every single audition you go to has the opportunity to be a learning experience and every one of those auditions that you are well prepared for increases your chances even further. Practicing more, learning more, studying more, and attending more auditions allows you to effectively buy many, many more "industry lottery tickets."

If you are skilled, driven, and willing, eventually your number will be called. The only way to fail in this industry is to give up.

85. Know when it's time to go back to your teacher

The good thing about this tip is that there is probably no such thing as a bad time to resume study with a trusted teacher! Some of my students almost never take any extended time off unless they're touring or traveling, in which case a lot of teachers, myself included, are only a video feed away should you need us. However, there are several limitations to "remote" lessons. With the current state of technology, one of the biggest is the inability to accompany singers on the piano simultaneously as they sing. Therefore, most songs need to be worked on using tracks, or sometimes even *a cappella*.

Some students, due to financial or time constraints, prefer to study intermittently and schedule a lesson only once in a while. So, if you fall into this category, how do you know when such a "need" has arisen?

Well, in a nutshell, it's a good time for an appointment whenever you're asked to do something you can't currently do, or, at the very least, do as easily or frequently as might be needed for a specific role. This might include singing in a style that you don't have a lot of experience in, singing in a higher or lower range than you perform comfortably, singing a more vocally vigorous part than you've attempted before, or if you're experiencing some new or unusual issues with your voice.

Also, if you are rarely, if ever, getting callbacks, it's a sure sign that you need to have a critical eye take a good close look at what your current strengths and weaknesses are. This will only help you in the long run.

You might also find a teacher's counsel helpful when you're stuck in a rut. For example, if you were able to book a steady stream of callbacks or jobs for a while but seem to be hitting a dry spell, I'd argue it's time for an outside set of ears. Remember what I said about creating a long, "committed" relationship with a teacher who knows you and your work well? One of the most valuable contributions your teacher can make to your overall development as an artist is that they are in the unique position to compare the current "you" to a former "you" who was less (or *more*) successful. What has changed in the time you've been on lesson sabbatical? Have aspects of your practice routine or vocal hygiene changed? Have you simply aged into a new category without even realizing it? It is never a fun thing to hear at first, though it is better to have someone who knows you well and cares for your well-being break this news. Or perhaps your overall appearance has altered, so a whole other category of roles might have recently opened to you?

Let someone who knows you, knows your voice, and knows your history help contextualize whatever you are dealing with today, and it is sure to make for a more productive tomorrow.

86. Respect the learning curve

Learning isn't a destination, but a journey. You always want to be learning new songs, new monologues, new dance steps, new musical genres, new instruments, new languages, new approaches to life. Sometimes you might have to take a brief break when you're mentally overloaded or have taken on a particularly demanding role (there's only so much new stuff most performers can realistically take on in one go).

Probably the moment you've mastered that new material, however, you'll want to go back to the studio and try out something else for the first time. Never, ever become complacent. There's lots of research to suggest that people with a lifelong commitment to learning and who are always trying new things make for the happiest adults with the best overall cognitive function into their twilight years. Look at some of our greatest living performers who continue to sing and act into well into their seventies, eighties, and beyond. They are, without question, continually curious and motivated learners.

Also, the practice of trying out new things makes it easier to fight perfectionistic tendencies if you tend towards that direction. Just the act of *being* a beginner at something new is one of the best ways for your ego to adapt to the idea that it's OK not to be an instant master at everything you try. By adopting the mindset of a perpetual student, the idea of a performance never being 100 percent perfect becomes more exciting than daunting. It means that not only is it okay to have a learning curve, but that every practice session is an opportunity to do something fantastic for the first time.

Major technical skills will often require many practice sessions, sometimes hundreds or thousands, depending on the complexity of the task. You might have noticed that some of the "keys" in this book are much easier said than implemented, and that a few of them will take you weeks or months just to begin to strategize solutions.

You just need to accept that it's going to take as long as it takes. The time you put into acquiring new skills will eventually pay off!

87. Embrace virtual learning

For a variety of reasons, you might decide to do some of your coaching and singing lessons with professionals who are located farther than you're able to travel. With continually improving technological advances, this is now a real alternative to live, in-person instruction. However, there are still some considerations to get the best results from online lessons.

Since current technology doesn't easily allow an accompanist to accompany a singer on the piano simultaneously, a second device is needed to playback piano tracks while singing. One device is used for the connection (desktop computer, laptop, tablet, etc.), and another to playback accompaniment tracks (smartphone, tablet, etc.) Your teacher might need to send over a track or two during the lesson, so hopefully whatever device is used for playback can receive text messages and/or emails. Some teachers advise using headphones and an external microphone, but I've had particularly good results using just the built-in speakers and microphones on our devices.

Prior to your first online lesson, you and your teacher will have to agree on which communication platform is best for both of you. You will also want to use the best internet Wi-Fi connection you can, and either get as close to the router as possible or plug your computer in directly via an Ethernet cable. You'll also want to disconnect other programs or applications that might interfere with the Wi-Fi connection.

Also, you'll want to perfect the art of auditioning online live or on video. Practice, independence, and ingenuity will go a long way toward making you feel comfortable in front of a microphone and camera. Having the means to record, edit, and send examples of your performances from your own home might make the difference when it comes to landing your next callback or performing job. Although your teachers and coaches are there as guides, the goal is for *you* to ultimately be able to continue to train, work, audition, and put your best foot forward as an artist.

88. And one to grow on

I wasn't kidding when I said I learn something every day and that I love to share what I'm learning. Even if this book hits the shelves next week, that means that I'll have stumbled across at least a half dozen pearls that I didn't know today! Feel free to follow me on Facebook, Twitter, or sign up for my e-newsletter at www.bobmarks.com to keep up with me and let me know what you're up to.

Chapter 10: Encore!
Additional Resources

Here are some additional pointers on how to keep your voice in top-notch shape from Voice Pathologist and "Vocal Athlete Expert," Dr. Wendy LeBorgne, Ph.D. CCC-SLP:

As a Vocal Athlete (singer or actor), you rely on your voice to be flexible, agile, have stamina, power, and consistency of performance. This is especially important when you are working to maintain an eight-show per week performance schedule. The reality is that not everything you do is going to be "vocally healthy." Still, it becomes vital to maximizing as many aspects of vocal health that you can control so that you can have vocal longevity and perform throughout your lifetime.

Below are some vocal wellness tips and recommendations for all vocal athletes to consider and implement into their practice and performance. Consider yourself as an Olympic-level athlete, with everything from physical fitness level, to mental wellness, exercises to warm-up/cool-down, foods you ingest and performing when you aren't feeling well are all aspects of training and vocal fitness.

Tips for Vocal Health & Wellness

1. **Train your voice and body just like an athlete:** Learn proper singing technique with a voice teacher, don't overuse the voice, get plenty of rest, and eat a balanced, healthy diet. Singers are like vocal gymnasts who traverse their artistic range with apparent ease and flexibility. Gymnasts are extremely disciplined people who spend hours perfecting their craft and are much more likely than the general public to sustain an injury. Professional singers carry some of these same risks and must maintain a disciplined training and practice schedule with intervals of rest and recovery to perform at an optimal level.

2. **Let your unique voice shine.** Attempting to imitate someone else's voice or singing style can require you to sing or do things outside of your comfortable physiologic range or current vocal skill level. This could result in vocal injury. Also, remember that if you are imitating someone already famous, their millions have been made. You want to be the next star that they hire, not just a copycat. This means training the healthiest YOU possible.

3. **Vocal Dose and Vocal Load.** When you are preparing for a show or audition season, you must pace yourself and your voice. You would not think of trying to get all of your exercise in at the gym by going one day a week for five hours. Rather, you should sing (and exercise)

in smaller increments of time (30-45 minutes) each day, gradually building muscular skill and stamina. As you improve, you should be able to increase the amount of time as well as the difficulty of vocal skill.

4. **Turn down the Vocal Volume!** Avoid yelling, screaming, loud talking, singing too loudly, and singing over the music in the car. When you increase your vocal loudness, your vocal folds bang together harder (much like clapping your hands hard, loud, and fast). After a period of doing this, your vocal folds begin to react to the impact by becoming swollen and red. Long-term phonotrauma can lead to vocal fold changes such as vocal fold nodules.

5. **Adequate hydration.** Be sure to drink plenty of non-caffeinated beverages throughout the day. Remembering that nothing you eat or drink gets onto the vocal folds (food and liquid go through the esophagus and into the stomach), adequate oral hydration allows the mucus to act like a lubricant instead of glue. You want to consider that it takes approximately two hours after you drink water (or any liquid) to get the systemic benefits of the water. Therefore, anything you drink during your show is likely not impacting the vocal folds themselves, but rather providing surface hydration to the mouth and pharynx (back of throat). Also, you should consider ingesting water-dense foods (e.g., cucumbers, watermelon, etc.) to add increased

hydration with minimal calories to your diet. Use a warm or cool humidifier if the air in your environment is especially dry as it provides added moisture to the air you breathe. Steamy showers and personal steamers are also beneficial for providing external moisture. However, this is not a replacement for oral hydration!

6. **Minimize Your Chance of Acid Reflux**. Many singers battle with acid reflux (which is small amounts of stomach acid regurgitating back into your esophagus–GERD, and sometimes your larynx–LPRD). Sometimes, you don't even know that you have reflux because you don't feel symptoms of heartburn. Symptoms of "silent reflux," also known as LPRD are hoarseness, longer warm-up time, loss of range, feeling a lump in the throat, sensation of post-nasal drip, and vocal fatigue. Tips to avoid reflux include: avoid spicy or acidic foods, stay upright for two to three hours after you eat, avoid clothes that are tight around the abdomen, and avoid coffee and alcoholic beverages. Yes, anything that tastes good is seemingly on this "do not do" list!

7. **Vocal Warm-ups and Vocal Cool Downs.** Singers are generally accustomed to warming up their voices before engaging in high demand vocal activities. Be sure that your vocal warm-ups are targeted to achieve your desired effect (e.g., stretching your frequency range, finding a perfect resonance). Don't forget to also warm up your body and breathing mechanism

through physical stretching and respiratory exercises. Remember that your vocal mechanism includes your whole body, and, as such, your warm-ups should be considered "whole body" warm-ups to get you ready to meet your performance demands. When you are done with your lesson or performance, you should consider vocal and physical "cool-downs." Similar to stretching following intense exercise, research on vocal cool-downs has demonstrated that singers have an easier time the following day returning to their singing activities in comparison to those singers who did not cool down. Consider vocal cool-downs as bringing your voice back to neutral after you have used it at its physiologic extremes during your lesson or performance.

8. **Butt Out!!!** Singers are well aware that smoking (including tobacco, marijuana, and vaping) are all bad for long-term vocal health. Beyond the known carcinogens, nicotine in cigarettes and formaldehyde in many of the vapes, the burning temperatures of cigarettes and marijuana are well above the boiling point of water. It is safe to say that no person would pour boiling water intentionally on their hands, so why, as a singer, would you consider inhaling at temperatures well above boiling over your vocal folds. The heat damage alone to the vocal fold mucosa is substantial and results in polypoid degeneration.

9. **Outside the Voice Studio.** Consider your speaking voice outside of your singing. Is your speaking voice well supported by your breath? Are you a "loud talker?" Singers will often have excellent control of their voices inside the voice studio or show, but when they speak, their voices are sub-optimal. Consider your vocal intensity. If you are a person that everyone can always hear across a room, that may not be a compliment, and you may need to consider turning it down a notch. Similarly, you want to optimize all of the elements of your speaking voice, just as you do in your singing voice (clear, resonant sound without glottal fry or uptalking). As most vocal athletes are "vocally enthusiastic" people by nature, consider taking vocal "naps" during your day – five to ten minutes every hour or two where you don't talk.

10. **The Show Must Go On Syndrome.** To sing or not to sing, that is often a concern of vocal athletes, because you will invariably get sick during the least appropriate time (such as just before opening night!). Performing during an illness can be a slippery slope. If you have throat pain or hoarseness, you should see your medical voice care specialist (ENT or Voice Pathologist), so they can evaluate whether it's safe to perform with your vocal situation. Sometimes, medications or a steroid may provide some relief of symptoms, but they could also give you a false sense of "being well" and you may over-sing, resulting in further vocal injury. Ultimately,

if you are sick, there is no show or role worth risking the rest of your career. None of your cast-mates want your illness, and sometimes rest is best. There are times when you must perform through an illness and, when you do, think of it as running on a sprained ankle: you learn to adjust and "get through." But if you do this time and time again, you will begin to develop new (often inappropriate) muscle patterns for voice production. It only takes one fall to break your leg and 10 weeks to get back to running. Consider this analogy when you are sick or vocally injured.

— Wendy D. LeBorgne, B.F.A., M.A., Ph.D. CCC-SLP

Dr. Wendy LeBorgne is a sought-after voice pathologist, international speaker, best-selling author, and master-class clinician regarding vocal wellness and vocal athletes. Dr. LeBorgne actively presents on the professional voice on vocal wellness. Her recent TED talk on Voice Branding™ enlightens audiences on the elements of authentic, engaged communication. She maintains a private studio (ProVoice Consultants), and her students currently can be seen and heard on radio, TV, film, cruise ships, Broadway, off-Broadway, national tours, commercial music tours, and opera stages around the world.

Reach out for more information on Dr. Wendy's services (www.drwendy.me) or connect with her (contact@drwendy.me)

Useful Websites

www.actorsaccess.com

www.backstage.com

www.denisesimoncoaching.com

www.drwendy.me

www.jenrudin.com

www.korovinmd.com

www.musicnotes.com

www.jenrudin.com

www.playbill.com

www.ncvs.org/rx.html

Acknowledgements

Over the years, I have accompanied thousands of singers during their auditions. I've witnessed many performers committing easy-to-correct mistakes, errors that might have prevented them from receiving a callback or, perhaps, even a coveted spot in a show. It occurred to me that I could reach and help more singers by sharing in a book what I've learned as an accompanist, musical director, voice teacher, and audition coach. The genesis of this book rests with Elizabeth Gerbi, a musical theatre professor, author, and pedagogue. After a few lunches, we created the book's outline and I'm forever indebted to her knowledge, creativity, and experience. I couldn't have done this without her.

Trying to piece together a lifetime of thanks is a daunting undertaking. My biggest fear is leaving out anyone who might have inadvertently escaped my memory. I'll begin by thanking my first "clients," including my sister, Lauren Greenberg, and musical classmates from John Bowne High School and Queens College. They willingly worked with me in my first "studio," which was in my parent's basement.

I never could have achieved any success without the patience, guidance, and generosity of many wonderful people. I must start with Beverly Ron, who directed a local production of *Damn Yankees* and took a chance on a 14-year-old novice musical director. The incredible performance teacher and author David Craig allowed me to audit his "Singing Onstage" performance classes, and became a friend as well as an advisor. Legendary Producer/Director/Professor Edward Greenberg had the faith to hire an unproven college student to assume the position of Associate Conductor of the largest outdoor theatre in the country. And thank you to pianist, orchestrator, and Broadway conductor Arnie Gross, who mentored me from high school through today, and is still my sounding board and good friend. His dad was my high school's music department chairman who connected us, and we've been friends for more than half a century!

Thank you, Joseph Schwartz, my high school English teacher, for allowing me to assume the position of musical director of his school repertory theatre group. The late Martin Charnin, lyricist and director of *Annie* included me in his projects wherever he could, and Max Morath was gracious enough to accept a phone call from an unknown teenaged piano player (me), who was infatuated with ragtime music. I'm proud that in later years, Max and I worked on several stage projects together.

My entire online presence, including my website, newsletters, and most of my printed material is the work of Jennifer LaPeruta, User Experience Professional. She is my friend, former client, and former stage mother, who is talented in both the visual and technical worlds; I'd be lost without her (www.jenniferlaperuta.com). I also need to acknowledge my friends Ethan Winer, who facilitated the digitalization of my studio, and Douglas Gorenstein, who photographed me even though I had serious doubts that I could ever look even acceptable in pictures. My incredible promotional video was conceived and edited by Allen Fawcett, Broadway's original Joseph in *Joseph and the Amazing Technicolor Dreamcoat*.

Thank you Nancy Carson (agent and author of *Raising a Star*) for your lovely forward to this book, your additional informative words about agents and managers, and your 40-plus years of friendship. I'm especially appreciative of you trusting me with your precious clients all this time.

I've been proud to co-teach many workshops with talented acting teachers, including Diane Hardin, Katie Cappiello, Samantha Simpson, Jen Rudin, and Denise Simon. Denise and I have taught side-by-side for many years. After her own book was published (*Parenting in the Spotlight*), Denise was kind enough to offer advice and motivation for me to write my own book. Most importantly, she introduced me to publisher Lynne Klippel. Lynne and her team have been the most encouraging, patient, creative, and responsive professionals an author could want. And thank you Lisa Sharkey, Danielle Cozart Steele, and Robert Edwin for reading early drafts of this book, and for your valuable editing and advice.

I'm humbled by the beautiful testimonials that begin this book. I consider my clients my friends, so it's especially gratifying to thank Alan Simon, Ben Lipitz, Denise Simon, Elizabeth Lecoanet, Jack Eppler, Laura Nevels, Lisa Ratner, Robert Doyle, Robert Edwin, Stephanie Lynne Mason, Tara Kennedy, Terri Troiano, Wayne Pyle, William W Wallace, and Audrey Heffernan Meyer for their kind words.

I thought it would be illuminating to include some audition stories from performers I've worked with over the years. I'm indebted to Amanda Foto, Celia Mei Rubin, Kathy Morath, Lauren Conley, Maureen Mershon, Michael Marotta, Peggy Lee Brennan, and Rusty Riegelman for adding their unique experiences to this book.

Thank you Janine Molinari, Jen Rudin, Dr. Wendy LeBorgne, and Dr. Gwen Korovin for offering your professional words of advice sprinkled among the chapters. I'd also like to acknowledge

Eric Brown, Bob Luke, Mark Meylan, Michele Sandler, Sue Winik, and Marilyn Zitner for their continued friendship and belief in the work I do.

Most of all, I'd like to thank YOU: whether you're my friend, participated in one of my classes, done a musical with me, sang in one of my cabaret showcases, studied with me in-person or online, or you're just reading this book, I appreciate you, and the fact is that without you, I've got nothing.

– *Bob Marks*
September 2020

About the Authors

Bob Marks

Bob Marks is a voice teacher, coach, conductor, arranger, and director, specializing in helping singers show their talents off to their best possible advantage. As a voice professional, his number one priority, now and always, has been vocal health. He works with singers of all ages, from absolute beginners to celebrities, and recently taught his 90,000th private session in his New York City studio.

Mr. Marks holds a degree in speech and voice pathology, and has taught at the American Musical & Dramatic Academy and the Weist-Barron School in New York. He has been Special Guest Instructor at the Contemporary Commercial Music (CCM) Vocal Pedagogy Institute at Shenandoah Conservatory in Virginia, The New York Singing Teachers' Association (NYSTA) Professional Development Program at Columbia University, The Voice Foundation Symposium: Care of the Professional Voice, and at NYU's Steinhardt School of Education. He has given workshops, master classes and seminars internationally. His articles have appeared in several publications, including the internationally recognized *Journal of Singing*.

For several years, he was the host and musical director of the acclaimed *Youngstars* cabaret performances of professional children in New York City. His music arrangements have been heard on many compact disc releases of the "Revisited" series of recordings on Painted Smiles Records. He also had the honor of directing ragtime legend Max Morath in *Ragtime and Again* off-Broadway at the York Theatre.

He has been the musical director of over 200 productions across the country, including every style of music, from *Kismet* to *The Rocky Horror Show*. He has coached cast members of almost every current Broadway musical, and former students have included Laura Bell Bundy, Kerry Butler, Debbie Gibson, Ariana Grande, Nikki M. James, Ricki Lake, Constantine Maroulis, Lea Michele, Sarah Jessica Parker, Natalie Portman, Christy Carlson Romano, Jamie-Lynn Sigler, Britney Spears, and Ashley Tisdale.

He was a pianist with the Broadway and national companies of the hit musical *Annie*, and spent two seasons as the Associate Conductor of the St. Louis Muny Opera, working with stars such as Shirley Jones, Paul Williams, Carol Lawrence, and Vincent Price.

At a time when all styles of non-classical music were mostly ignored and misunderstood by singing teachers, Mr. Marks helped found the seminal Music Theatre Committee of NYSTA, which continues to be a key element in its programs. For over 30 years, he has maintained a private voice and recording studio in midtown Manhattan. He is a member of American Society of Composers, Authors, and Publishers (ASCAP); New York Singing Teachers' Association (NYSTA); National Association of Teachers of Singing (NATS); and the National Academy of Recording Arts & Sciences (NARAS).

Contact Bob through his website, www.BobMarks.com

Elizabeth Gerbi

Elizabeth Gerbi is a Full-Time Instructor of Musical Theatre at the State University of New York at Dutchess Community College and proud member of the College Music Teaching Summer Doctoral Cohort at Teachers-College-Columbia University. She holds additional degrees in Music Performance and Music Education from Boston University and Ithaca College School of Music. She is well known across the country as a singing teacher, voice coach, conductor, and music director/pianist, having worked on over 200 musicals regionally and in the greater New York City area.

As a versatile singer-actor, she has appeared in regional productions ranging from *I Pagliacci* to *Les* Misérables to *The Kenny Rogers Christmas Tour*. Projects include music directing *The Chris Betz Show* (Rose's Turn/Sage Theatre, NYC), *Side Show* and *Tommy* (Westchester Broadway Theatre), *Seussical* (Debaun Auditorium), and *The Sound of Music* (Wagon Wheel Theatre, Warsaw, IN). She has accompanied master classes for Broadway performers such as Ken Jennings, Lisa Howard, Denise Summerford, and Lindsay Mendez, adapting *Starmites* for Broadway composer Barry Keating, and recently completed a European tour with her husband (and favorite collaborator), Christopher Brellochs, performing at venues such as the prestigious Paris Conservatoire at St. Maur and Saint Marri.

As a rising musical theatre scholar, pedagogue, and author, she has published several peer-reviewed articles in the National Association of Teachers of Singing *Journal of Singing* and the *Journal of the Musical Theatre Educators' Alliance*. She has also taught workshops for developing artists at the International Thespian Festival and Educational Theatre Association, Kennedy Center American College Theatre Festival, New York State Theatre Education Association, and New England Theatre Conference, and has regularly presented papers and participated on panels for the Association for Theatre in Higher Education. Her continuing scholarship is focused upon creating more inclusive pathways into the musical theatre industry, particularly through the implementation of two-year musical theatre programs at the community college level to cultivate new and diverse talent. For more information, please visit www.elizabethgerbi.com

Made in the USA
Monee, IL
13 May 2021